Praise for The Emergen

"NNNN", "Brutally honest, macabre and often hilarious..."
-Jordan Bimm (NOW Magazine)

"VVVV", "Blood, guts, feces, severed testicles, no body part is spared..."
- The Varsity

"Four stars", "Morgan Jones Phillips is a natural storyteller and a total dude...hilarious, cringe worthy anecdotes..."
-Paul Gallant (EYE WEEKLY)

"Top Five plays of The 2009 Toronto Fringe Festival"
-Kaori Furue (Torontoist)

"At times touching and at times hysterically funny, 'The Emergency Monologues' pulls back the curtain to reveal a world in which paramedics must deal on a daily basis with situations tragic and funny. Phillips brings his biting wit and keen sense of observation into a funny and compelling book that should be required reading for anyone who imagines themselves picking up the phone and dialing '911' one day."

-Dr. Brian Goldman, MD. Host of White Coat, Black Art *on CBC radio and author of* Night Shift: Real Life in the Heart of the ER

"Your show was awesome. I can't wait to see another one. To everyone that needs a laugh, (which is everyone out there) buy the book and I guarantee your face will hurt from laughing!!!"

-Mike Moran (40 station Paramedic)

"Morgan Jones Phillips is big and friendly and tells funny and horrifying stories from his work as a paramedic, and he has all the unnerving, loquacious energy of the shell shocked."

-Evan Webber (Time and Space)

"Phillips neatly mixes humour and personal commentary with some dead-serious topics. He's a charming storyteller and knows how to improvise if the occasion arises, though the material would probably work better over a few shared drinks than in the theatre."

-Jon Kaplan (NOW Magazine)

"The Emergency Monologues drove away with the NOW Audience Choice Award."

-NOW Magazine

"Side-splittingly hilarious view into the world of Paramedicine"

-Jason Ng (FNG)

"...gruesome, hilarious and not to be missed."

-BlogTO.com

"As you read 'Emergency Monologues' prepare to be doubled over with laughter. Morgan Jones Phillips is witty and observant in this excellent account of what 'really goes on' in the life of a paramedic."

-Dr. Vincent Lam, MD. Author of the Giller Award winning Bloodletting and Miraculous Cures.

"Phillips [has an] easy and unaffected knack for telling funny as hell stories about crime scenes and head-on collisions."

-Sean Davidson (EYE WEEKLY)

"I loved your book!!! SO good. When I saw your Summerworks show I felt like I wanted it to be three hours longer than it was, and the book is like getting that wish."

-Zoe Whittall, author of Bottle Rocket Hearts *and* Holding Still For as Long as Possible

"This would make great bathroom reading."

-Paul Butters (ex-guitarist, Endsville)

"It's already in my bathroom."

-Matthew Bartram (ex-keyboardist, Endsville)

"I might actually read this."

-Jules Phillips (brother of Morgan)

"…once he's in full flow he's an accomplished storyteller. The Emergency Monologues gives you glimpses of sights you pray you'll never have to witness for yourself. But there is more going on here than just a series of horror stories and gallows humour."

-Andrew Templeton (Plank Magazine)

"4.5 stars" (out of 5)

-www.goodreads.com

"(The alternate choice to one of) Five plays that could well live up to their hype."

-Globe and Mail

"A superb play that shows exactly how it is to be a front-line worker in the high-stress world of delivering emergency medical care in a uncaring city. Emergency Monologues is a fantastic read."

-Declan Hill, author of The Fix: Soccer and Organized Crime.

"Morgan Jones Phillips is a consummate story-teller –filling in the small details of each scenario as skillfully as a master-weaver entwines a rich tapestry."

-Luc Iogna (Director)

"If you've ever heard a siren in the night and wondered where it was going, The Emergency Monologues is your answer... Fascinating, gruesome, and laugh-out-loud funny."

-Chris Earle (Writer/performer of Radio:30 and *director/performer with Second City)*

"...hilarious, stomach-churning tales... If it is true that laughter is the best medicine, then anyone in the crowd with ailments must have gone home feeling a bit better, as heaping doses of hilarity were served."

- Shelley P Jones (Snap Bloor West)

"My favorite so far (at the Toronto Fringe Festival) is *The Emergency Monologues*, written and performed by the talented Morgan Jones Phillips. Excellent writing, skilled delivery and an outstanding stage presence make *The Emergency Monologues* work."

-Buck's Blog

"Funny and gruesome."

-Toronto.com

"That show was so frickin' funny, I'm still smiling. I haven't had such a good laugh in a while, felt almost medicinal...
So, thanks for that."

-Dr. Jacob Pendergrast, MD
(he's a doctor, trust him)

Suzie,
Sorry to hear about your accident. Heal up.

The Emergency Monologues

Enjoy some stories of someone else for a change.

By Morgan Jones Phillips
and
Illustrated by Vince Cheng

This book is a work of fiction and is intended to be enjoyed as such. As in all fiction, some literary perceptions and insights are based on experience and inspired by true-life events; however, all names, places, characters and incidences are either products of the author's imagination or are used fictitiously. Some characters are inspirations or composites of characters from life in general and are not meant to reflect any specific individuals. No reference to any real person living or dead is intended or should be inferred as all identifiable details have been changed to protect the identity of those involved. 'Nuff said.

The opinions expressed in this book are entirely those of the author and by no means reflect the opinions of other paramedics or the policies of TEMS; especially regarding firefighters.

If you see the name "Lukie" randomly placed in this book, it was my son. I left my computer open and he peppered his name throughout. I think I found them all, but let me know if I missed one.

Front cover and bio photo by John Phillips.
Back cover photo by the ever-awesome Michael Barker
(www.michaelbarker.ca)

First edition with illustrations. Fourteenth Printing otherwise.
1 of 100, September 2013. Toronto, ON.

To book a show, or just say "Hi", write anytime.
morganjonesphillips@gmail.com
Twitter: @emergemonos
Facebook/Emergency Monologues
www.emergencymonologues.com

Thanks to Pierre, Candy, Amanda, Jeff, Geoff, John, Jon and all the other wonderful partners I've had. My apologies to those I had when I was new. We all were once.

Special thanks to Marcel Rasile who was my preceptor in Durham. I was a fragile student when I met him, and he made all the difference in the world to me. Without him, I wouldn't be a paramedic today (take that as you will). Also, super-special thanks to Leo for being the best supervisor ever. He probably wouldn't want this to be common knowledge, but without him, I'd most likely have been fired by now.

Love and thank you to my Mom, Dad and Brothers (step et al) for endless support; and to both my Grandmothers (Jean and Kitty), who are still a constant source of inspiration.

Awesome high-fives to Evalyn Parry, Matthew Bartram, Jane Angel, Kaleigh O'Brien and others for reading, editing and/or giving advice on these stories in advance. Any errorz at this point are entirely mines,

A tip of the hat to all the great Paramedics and Emergency Medical Dispatchers working for TEMS; we keep it together. I'm 45, Schedule 1, Red now, but I'll always have a soft spot for SE Green and all at 40 Station.

A salute to all Paramedics, EMTs, Ambulance Personnel, Emergency First-Responders and First-Aiders everywhere.
Congratulations for doing what you do.

The Emergency Monologues was first performed at Theatre Passe Muraille Backspace as part of the SummerWorks Theatre Festival. It was directed by Evalyn Parry and performed by Morgan Jones Phillips from August 7-17 of 2008.
He worked three night shifts during the run.

The Emergency Monologues was remounted at The George Ignatieff Theatre for the 2009 Toronto Fringe festival. He worked two night shifts during this run.

Lidia, Zenon, Lukie, and Zoriana☺
You are all my everything, always.

For my Dad,
who made me who I am.

For my Mom and Grandma Jean,
who showed me that it is never too late to start writing your own stories.

Rebecca and Jamie,
and
Kevin and Heather.

Four of the bravest people I know,
who dealt with two of the shittiest
hands ever dealt to anyone.

Table of Contents

The following stories have been adapted from the largely improvised versions that were created onstage. They are not intended to be performed in the order presented in this text, though it wouldn't hurt. In a one-hour play it is impossible to tell every one of these stories. It is the author's intention that each performance contains different stories in a different order provided by The Wheel of Misfortune. This makes a unique theatrical experience for each audience and keeps it fresh for the performer. Miniature Wheels are not provided with the book, so you can read it however you like.

In some early editions XXX may appear alongside a heading or in the body of the text. It does not denote sexual or controversial stories. It is only a message to me (the author) that the story isn't quite finished to my satisfaction and that I need to come back to it. Stories of a sexual or controversial nature come with no warning.

The Emergency Monologues

By Morgan Jones Phillips
and
Illustrated by Vince Cheng

The stage is empty except for a large raffle wheel labeled with stories and a stool with 2 beer bottles and a glass of water. The wheel is labeled with the headings of the stories. Each time the wheel is spun, the marker will point to a different story and that story will be told. After every story the wheel is spun again. The performer is allowed some flexibility with the order of stories to allow for pacing, repeats, and finishing on time: a flexibility that will surely be exercised.

The performer enters the stage in a full mock paramedic uniform. He smiles to the audience, walks over to the wheel and spins it. No matter what it lands on he continues to turn the wheel until it points to Introduction.

Introduction

In 2003, when I first started working as a paramedic, every call I did was *SO* cool. Driving lights-and-sirens through the city, going into the subway to wake up a drunk guy, even taking an old lady to the hospital because she hadn't pooed in three days; it was all fresh and exciting and I wanted some record of it. I wanted to document it, not only for myself, but also for my children. I have three kids and I wanted them to know what kind of an exciting job their father had when they were young; however, as you are about to see, these tales don't make for very good children's bedtime stories.

I still write stories down but you should know that most of the stories in this show are from my first year on the job. I'm not trying to say that I'm jaded or burnt out and crispy, because after seven years in EMS, I still barely have my feet wet. Some guys have been on for 30 years and, in their eyes, anything under 10 years is still new. It may be embarrassing to say, but I still love my job. The thrill however, of going into Allen Gardens and trying to figure out which sleeping drunk man the drive-by caller on a cell phone was so worried about has lost its romance.

You'll notice that there are about 45 stories on the Wheel. Obviously, we aren't going to have time to tell them all. The way this will work is that I'll spin the wheel and we'll let Fate and the Wheel of Misfortune decide which stories get told tonight. There is a bit of risk involved for me because, very much like my job, I don't know what is going to come up next, so I can't really plan it out. I can't promise the smoothest transitions and the best segues. I can't promise a proper dramatic arc or the appropriate dénouement. At this point, I'm just hoping it isn't one dead baby story after another. There is also some risk for you, because you paid to watch me take this risk. So, very much like life, we're all in this together. And, much like life, I think it will be okay.

He makes a grand gesture to spin the wheel, but only turns it one click so that it points to Disclaimer.

Disclaimer

The opinions expressed in this play are solely those of the author and in no way reflect the opinions, values, polices and standard operating procedures of any EMS service. The behaviour portrayed by paramedics in these stories is by no means a reflection of appropriate behaviour condoned or encouraged by any EMS service. The names, addresses, dates, much of the facts and any identifying features around the patients have been changed to protect their identity.

You will notice that I often refer to my 'partner'. Please note that it isn't the same partner every time. If it is relevant to the story, I will let you know, but usually I won't, because I don't remember who it was. When you're new, you work with a different person almost every day.

Finally, let's just say these stories are all fictional. It all comes from my imagination for your enjoyment and they in no way represent anyone living or dead.

I'm ready to start if you are.

He now spins the wheel freely and fate takes over. Enjoy

Italian Open Fracture

We get a call for a 71-year-old man who had fallen down the stairs at home. It comes in as a Delta, which means a very high priority.

The inside is classically old-world European: wood paneling, flowery wallpaper, thick carpet, ceramic statues of animals and glass blown fish on the shelves and posters from the Pope's visit in 2002. It is the home of, if not your own parents, then one of your friends' parents growing up. Other than the regularly updated Pope's visit poster, the house hasn't been redecorated since the 1950s.

We arrive and find him at the bottom of the stairs in the basement. He is on his left side, all crumpled up and bleeding heavily from his left arm. It's an open fracture to the forearm so the bone is sticking out and nothing is holding the wrist and arm together except skin. A firefighter is holding the man's head in case there is a spinal injury from the fall. I tell the patient to hold very still while I assess for a possible c-spine injury. C-spine is clear so I tell the firefighter to release his head and I start doing my thing.

A broken arm, though visually spectacular, isn't necessarily that serious, but if the pain and distress triggers a heart attack, the acuity of the situation escalates very quickly. I'm asking about his past medical history and discover, as I predicted, that there is a language barrier. He's Italian and doesn't speak English very well so I'm not getting clear answers. I decide the best approach is for me to get his medication so I can play detective and figure out his history.

"Sir. Medicine. Where is your medicine?"

He starts gesturing with his hands.

"There," he says, pointing towards the kitchen. His floppy arm swings madly and blood sprays all around us.

"Sir. Don't move that arm. Are you alone in the house?"

"No," he replies. "Wife-a uppa stairs-a." And again he's swinging his arm all around gesturing up the stairs.

"Sir, don't move that arm. Is there a backdoor, or do we have to carry you up the stairs?"

"Back-a door-a." Again he's swinging his floppy arm around while pointing at the back of the house. I'm dodging blood like I'm in the Matrix. I finally tell a firefighter to hold his arm and not let him move. The firefighter is holding the arm still, but by now the patient has spun the limb into such a knot that it is looking disturbingly unnatural. It looks like someone stuck a glove on a pretzel. I see the firefighter's cheeks puff up and release in short bursts. His shoulders are twitching and he appears to be suppressing the urge to vomit.

"Look away," I suggest. Fortunately for all of us, he takes my advice.

Dislocated Shoulder

It's a warm summer night at around 2:00am when we get a call for a 17-year-old male with shoulder pain. The call information asks that we not use the lights and sirens. It's two o'clock in the morning on a residential street in Forest Hill for a Bravo: a medium priority call. I wouldn't be using the lights and sirens anyway, but now I'm tempted to. It's not like I go to his work and tell him when his burgers are ready to flip.

We arrive at the house and it is huge. It's a giant, fancy (Forest-Hill-fancy) house. Standing on the porch is a 17-year-old woman wearing an oversized t-shirt, men's boxer shorts and bare feet.

She walks out to meet us at the ambulance and explains that her boyfriend has hurt himself upstairs. She asks us if we can be very, very quiet because her parents are asleep and they don't know that he's there. My partner and I were both teenagers once and have climbed in and out of a few windows in our time, so in an effort to pay back some karma, we agree.

We creep into her home bringing only the bags we need to assess the situation. Her room is on the third floor. As we tiptoe past the second floor, she points to a door and whispers, "my parents".

"Okay," we mouth back to her.

It's a classic teenager's room. There are posters all over the walls and clothes all over the floor. Her bed is in the middle of the room where her boyfriend is laying face down wearing only his underwear. His arm is fixed straight up along his right ear and his elbow is bent so that his forearm runs over his head and gives the appearance that he's tapping himself on the shoulder. It is obviously dislocated. He is in a tremendous amount of pain and can't move.

It takes all of my will power not to ask how it got dislocated. In my mind I imagine the questions that I *could* be asking him, "What were you doing when it popped out? It's important that I know the exact position you were in when it came out of joint." It's tempting, but I don't ask.

With the boyfriend in great agony we struggle to get him off the bed. If you've ever dislocated a limb, or been with someone who has, then you know how tremendously painful it is. These patients are usually screaming uncontrollably, but this guy is being stone silent. He is doing a fantastic job of stifling his screams. I comment on how quiet he is being and how much I appreciate it.

"This shoulder is nothing compared to what my girlfriend's parents will do to me if I'm caught up here in my underwear." Having a daughter myself, I don't doubt it.

With time, and enormous pain on his part, we get him standing at the foot of the bed. He looks woozy and says that he doesn't feel well. He starts to feel dizzy and tells us he wants to lie down. We desperately try to remind him how hard it was to get him standing and that he'll have to go through all that pain again if he lies back down. He starts to sway on the balls of his feet. The pain has overwhelmed him and it appears that he is going to faint.

Instead of fainting, he projectile vomits all over the room. It is an incredibly impressive mess that unfortunately includes my partner's shoes. As soon as he is finished tossing his cookies, the patient looks around as if seeing with glasses for the first time. "I feel a lot better," he says. "In fact, I'm okay." He starts moving his arm around freely. His shoulder was successfully popped back into place by a therapeutic hurl. "Yeah, I'm fine. Thanks guys," he says looking at his girlfriend hungrily and wiping the vomit from his chin. "I don't want to go to the hospital."

My partner picks up a shirt from the floor, wipes his shoes, turns to me and says softly, "I'll be in the truck."

We sneak out as carefully as we came in. Well, *I* am being as quiet as I can, but I notice that my partner's shoes fall a little heavier on the stairs and he bangs a few walls, including the parents bedroom, with the cardiac monitor on the way out.

We fully expect that if her parents noticed us leaving, we'll get a call later that night to the same address for a 17-year-old male in his underwear thrown out a third story window.

Assault/Buying Crickets

The first rule of any first aid class is to 'check your environment'. You have to make sure the scene is safe before you go in. It's common sense. You can't help someone else if you hurt yourself in the process and you're certainly no good to the patient if you're dead. When a call comes in for an assault, we wait for the police in case the assailant is still on scene. A few years ago a paramedic supervisor was shot at, his car hit twice (no, a road medic wasn't the shooter). I've also had friends walk into the middle of an attempted murder scene without knowing the assailant was still there. Sometimes the only difference between assault and murder is time and enthusiasm.

We also wait for police if the problem is unknown. For example, if you call 911 and say, "Send an ambulance quick!!!" and then hang up, I guarantee that it won't come quick. For all the 911 call-taker knows, you've been shot and the guy with the shotgun is downstairs wanting to kill anyone who tries to save your life. We'll wait outside, often down the street, and go in with the police when they arrive. The police can deal with the shooter and we can deal with the shootee. Usually, it turns out not to be a dangerous situation and I feel bad wasting the cop's time, but it could save my life and I don't want my kids to be the subject of an after school special.

So I'm in uniform buying crickets for my bearded dragon at the Menagerie pet store on Parliament. I love completing any errand while on the job, but I especially love picking up crickets. The way they chirp in the ambulance always gets an interesting reaction from the patients. Especially from patients having psychiatric emergencies and *especially* when I deny hearing anything.

I like it too because if you are at a stand-by and you close your eyes, you can sit in the truck and imagine that you are in a field somewhere. Very pastoral. Very relaxing.

The pet-store-guy is scooping crickets and putting them in a bag for me when my pager goes off. I read it out loud. “Assault. 2 men. Knives involved. No further information. Police not yet on scene.” The address was at the apartment building right across the street. We are so close that I know if I left right away I’d get there before the police. In fact, my partner is most likely watching the whole thing go down.

The guy turns to look at me, “Oh my God. Do you have to go?”

“No, no,” I reply, “I’ve got time. I’ve also got a hungry lizard at home. Just keep filling that bag with crickets.”

Priorities are important.

OH GOOD! YOU GUYS ARE HERE! MY WIFE IS IN LABOUR!!
UH... I THINK I READ ABOUT DELIVERING A BABY, **ONCE**
THANK GOD IT'S YOUR TURN TO ATTEND! I'LL SEE YOU BACK AT THE TRUCK
AAAHHHHHH! THE BABY'S COMING!! I HAVE TO PUSH!!
I JUST HEARD A SPLASH. DID MY WIFE'S WATER BREAK?
NO, I JUST PEE'd MYSELF IN ANTICIPATION OF HAVING TO DELIVER A BABY
IT POPPED OUT IN THE BACK OF THE AMBULANCE! NOW WHAT DO I DO WITH IT!?!
JUST HAND ME THE BABY, MORGAN...

Rules of Paramedicine/Things That Amaze Me

Some are adapted from a locker magnet I once saw.

1. People die.
2. You can't always change rule #1.
3. Anything blue on a patient is bad.
4. Air goes in and out and blood goes round and round. Any variation on this is bad.
5. If it's after midnight at an MVC (motor vehicle collision) and nobody's drunk, there is someone missing.
6. Never say, "Holy Shit!" when taking someone's blood pressure or looking at the cardiac monitor.
7. An unconscious patient is a compliant patient.
8. Carbon Dioxide works faster than midazolam. Or, if you don't have time to subdue a violent patient medically, you can always strangle them. The end result is similar.
9. All bleeding stops, eventually.
10. After a delivery, if you drop the baby, pick it up.
11. You call, we haul. You ring, we bring. It's no more than a Cab-ulance. Just do the call. Nobody ever got fired for bringing someone to the hospital.
12. People who drink Listerine **don't** smell minty-fresh.
13. People who OD on Gravol vomit... a lot
14. When your supervisor shows up with an incident report, say you were the driver.
15. In an apartment building, the patient will always be at the end of the hallway, usually on the left.
16. When you pull up behind a car with the lights and sirens on, the car will behave in the most unpredictable way possible.

17. People who threaten to leave the Emerge unless they are seen ASAP will have their charts moved to the bottom of the pile.
18. Drunks who can't stand on their own will want to fight you when you help them up.
19. The same drunk who tells you to 'fuck off' and then takes a swing at you will ask you for a cigarette.
20. People with a minor problem will get irate about other people clogging the Emergency Department.

Jokes

These may not read funny, but I'm telling you, these jokes go over well said aloud to an unsuspecting victim. At least, they go over well to me. I fully acknowledge that I've begun telling "Dad jokes" which embarrass my kids. These probably fit into that category of groaning jokes, but you've got to try them on someone. I never get tired of the first one. If you aren't a paramedic, you can always adapt it to say that you read it in the paper.

#1 Film Fest

"I did a stabbing during the Film Fest for one of the actresses. She was eating a bowl of yoghurt on a patio in Yorkville when a guy came up behind her and stabbed her in the shoulder. It was… Oh what's her name? Big star… Reese…" (*pause to let the other person say 'Witherspoon?'*) "No. He didn't use her spoon, he used his own knife to do it."

Other Jokes, not in show

These were left out of the show, but they make me laugh so I put them in the book.

#2 **Henway**

"I did this crazy call for a guy who actually choked on a henway."
(*The other person usually asks, "What's a henway? To which you respond…*)
"About 2 pounds."

#3 **DeMann**

(To a partner who is a male)
Me: They want to split us up for the night. They want you to work with DeMann (*made up person, he doesn't exist, so he will reply…*)
Him: Who's DeMann?
Me: You DeMann, buddy. You the man.

#4 **Miegrill** ("My-Grill")

(*to a partner who is female*)
Me: You hear that we're getting a new supervisor. They're sending us Miegrill. (*again this is a made up person, so she will reply…*)
Her: Who's Miegrill?
Me: C'mon. You my girl, baby. You know that.

I feel like I should apologize for these jokes. Let me just say that sometimes you get giddy on a night shift and I shouldn't be given access to a computer.

Achilles' Tendon/Photos Taken of Me

I've had my photo taken a few times on calls and, as far as I know, it was never for the media. My dad used to call me every time a bald, bearded, bespectacled paramedic was on the news doing a call. He would ask if it was me, but so far, it never has been.

The first time someone pulled out a camera, I was on a call for a 60-year-old male injured during a basketball game. We arrive and the man is lying on the ground screaming in pain. His Achilles' tendon has ruptured. It's very painful with very bad consequences. He tells me that he had promised his wife that he would quit playing basketball when he turned 60 and today is his birthday, so this was to be his last game. Unfortunately, with a torn Achilles he's *really* going to quit playing.

While we're packaging him up he asks if his friends can take a picture. I agree thinking that it will be an action shot as we wrap him up and splint his leg. Suddenly everyone is gathering around me for a posed shot of him. People on either side of me are putting their arms around me. He stops screaming and has a giant smile on his face. We take a group shot of him on the stretcher with all his friends and family gathered around. Everyone is smiling and he is lying on the stretcher in the middle of all of us. He e-mailed me the picture later. It's brilliant! You have no idea what kind of agony he is in.

The second time a camera made an appearance was while I was sitting in offload delay at Scarborough General. Scarborough Gen has two waiting rooms: both are public but most people only know about one of them. Paramedics tend to gather in the other one.

We had been sitting for hours waiting for a bed along with six other crews. The sister of our patient took a picture: two rows of seats all filled with paramedics watching TV, while stretchers and patients are spread around the sides. The patients who aren't too gorked out are arranged so that they can also see the TV. The gorked out ones are closer to the walls or under the TV. They can't open their eyes and therefore don't need the view.

The most recent photo was at a house party on New Year's Eve. Hundreds of 20 year olds with at least seven kegs are visible on the lawn alone. Everyone is drunk, and everyone is nubile. One girl tripped just as another fell on her. This broke her wrist. My partner is assessing the patient and I am doing crowd control keeping the apologetic, the curious and the "helpful" away from the patient.

A young girl comes up to me, points to another young girl and says, "She likes men in uniform." Then she points to another woman and says, "She likes men in uniform too." Then another says, "Give me a New Year's kiss." I look around and everyone has a camera phone and is taking pictures of the poor woman with the broken wrist who doesn't feel a thing because she is so drunk. "How about a hug?" I reply.

Code 5 = Very, Very, Very Dead

A Code 5 is what we call someone who is very, very dead. Mostly dead we can work with, but very, very dead is someone obviously beyond hope. In this case we do little to disturb the body because any Code 5 is a potential crime scene until police rule it out. The criteria to declare a patient Code 5 is any one of the following:

Decapitated. One rarely gets better after having his or her head chopped off. Even if you quickly try to screw it back on.

Transected through the Torso
When your top half and bottom half go in opposite directions, this is bad and very hard to fix. No amount of lining up organs, blood vessels and nerve endings will ever be good enough; especially, if you are trying to do this in the back of the ambulance.

Decomposing.

If the patient is rotting, this is a sure sign of being dead a long time. There are a few ways that people decompose, but the big dividing factor is: wet or dry. Dry is terrific, but more rare. The patient is more a leathery mummification and looks almost fake. Wet is a different story, though still looks kind of fake. First the patient bloats and then melts. This is especially horrible as a person contains a lot of water. Just imagine dumping 175 litres of goo on the floor. It spreads.

Dependent lividity.
When the heart stops beating, the blood tends to pool in the body, gravity side down, and makes a purplish bruising on whatever part of the body is closest to the Earth. By measuring how extensive the lividity is, you can determine how long someone has been dead through a formula with the air temperature. This knowledge will enrich your CSI watching.

Rigor mortis.

This is when, after death, the body becomes rigid, which is where the term "stiff" for a dead person comes from. There are waves of rigor that come and go. It always starts in the jaw, so the first thing we do with a newly dead person is try to wiggle their jaw. I don't know about you, but I've seen too many horror movies to wiggle the jaw without fear. I'm not going to lie, I asked my partner to hold my hand once at an especially gruesome Code 5. You just never know when the zombie apocalypse is going to start.

Exposed brain matter.

These are your gunshots, subway jumpers, falls from great heights and major car accidents. One usually doesn't live without parts of their brain for very long, although this doesn't explain Rob Ford, so perhaps one can live longer than previously believed.

Paramedics love Code 5s. They are always interesting because you get to play CSI and try to guess what happened. After concluding that they are Code 5, you don't have to touch them. These are always low stress calls because there is no hurry since they're already dead and they don't tend to get any worse. Sometimes we'll spend hours in a house or apartment with a Code 5. We can't leave until the police arrive and they aren't always available right away. It starts out creepy being in a house alone with a dead body, but pretty soon you get used to it and you're watching their TV and playing find the porn[·].

[·] "Find the porn" is an expression and should not be perceived as a game. While on scene, we need to search for medicine and medical information about the patient. *Sometimes,* we come across porn. **Believe me**, the last thing we would want to do would be to touch said porn. Think about it, you know where it's been. Gross. We would never intentionally look for anything that wasn't medically related. Hear that pitter-patter, that's the sound of thousands of men running around right now relocating their porn.

Check Address/Bad Smell in Hallway

We get a call for a check-address in an apartment building. A check-address is usually called in by someone from out of town. Generally, the story is that someone speaks regularly with a friend or relative by phone, but hasn't heard from them in a while. When they don't answer their phone, we go to see if they are dead.

A check-address always goes one of two ways: either they answer the door wearing a towel and say, "I was just in the shower and didn't hear the phone. My nephew always overreacts. Why are the police here? Why is he holding a piece of chalk?" or the person is dead and rotting.

The police always come because of the high likelihood that if the patient is Code 5, it might be a crime scene. The superintendent is also called because the dead rarely leave the door unlocked or come to let you in. Today is no different. We meet in the lobby and proceed to the elevator. As we step off the elevator and into the hallway my partner, the cop and I all smell the Code 5. It's obvious. Wordlessly we look at each other and prepare ourselves. I'm amazed that other people on the floor don't complain about the smell. It is so clear and distinct, but I guess if you didn't know what it was, you would think that it was a generic very bad smell and not your rotting neighbour.

We knock on the door. As expected, there is no answer. We knock again and just as I'm telling the super that we need him to unlock it, the door opens. The cop, my partner and I are all visibly startled. We jump a little higher than the average person does when a door is opened. The super probably thinks that we drink too much coffee. We quickly double-check the address. It is correct. An elderly person tells us that his phone hasn't been working but all is well. We step into his apartment for a quick sniff to make sure that he hasn't killed the resident and assumed his identity. With a tentative whiff we realize that the smell is definitely not coming from his apartment. We apologize and leave.

We discretely sniff each door as we walk back to the elevator. One of the ones in the middle definitely smells a little stronger than the others. Now, this is the situation: we know that there is a dead body in one of these apartments; we also know that it's 6:30pm and we all finish our shift at 7:00pm. None of us wants to get sucked into a time consuming Code 5. We know that this person is beyond saving and, therefore, not getting any worse so we ever-so-casually mention to the super that he might want to check on the other residents in that hallway sometime soon - but not in the next half hour.

Again, priorities.

Smells

I often get asked to name the worst thing I've ever seen. But dude, I'm here to tell you, it's not about what I've *seen*, it's about what I've **smelled**. I've smelled things that would turn your hair white. I don't even want to think about some of the particles that have wafted into my lungs. In college they don't prepare you for the things you're going to smell. And I don't just mean dead people. Dead people, or at least Code-5-very-dead-people, have a very distinct (and unpleasant) smell. If you didn't know what it was, you might just think it was the smell of garbage or rotting meat, which is exactly what it is. Once you know it though, you can't miss it. You'll easily pick it out of a whole selection of disgusting smells.

Dead people can smell pretty bad, but the living are even worse. With very dead people, you can keep your distance and leave them be. The living, however, often need to get picked up. You have to touch them to take their vital signs. You have to actually put your arms around them to lift them onto the stretcher.

Old urine is probably my personal choice for the worst smell. When someone has been lying in their own piss for a few days, and you move them for the first time, the aroma hits you like a sledgehammer. A sledgehammer wrapped in dirty socks, soaked in the urine of fifty tomcats living on an asparagus farm and then left in the back seat of a Yugo for the hottest week of the summer.

I have a friend who tried to tell me that she could feel my pain regarding urine soaked patients. She taught preschool and kindergarten and was telling me that pee soaked children was a major part of her work. It was a nice try but not the same. Fresh little-child-apple-juice-pee just isn't the same fluid as week-old, old-man-pee. No comparison.

Fresh vomit is pretty bad too. You'd think that someone who had been drinking Listerine would have minty-fresh puke, but surprisingly, it doesn't work that way. Ask any downtown paramedic if they use Listerine and they will probably say that they can't stand the smell. It triggers too many flashbacks. You know how if you have a lot of garlic, it starts to sweat out your pores? Same thing happens with Listerine.

Another nightmarish occupational hazard that one comes across is shit. Fresh or old, you really have no winning situation. Often it is dry and crusted under their fingernails. Their hand will be reaching up in slow motion to touch you as you're lifting them and there is nothing you can do about it but be touched or drop them. This may seem like an obvious choice and I'll admit I have 'slipped' my grasp on a few people to avoid contact, but generally professionalism rules and I suffer through having my cheeks stroked by someone who is a distant stranger to soap. Afterwards, I immediately reach for our most powerful disinfecting solution and Virox my face until the skin peels off.

It's like a horror movie where the poor bastard struggles with a bodiless arm that is possessed by a demon. Only this demon doesn't want to kill you, it wants to hold your hand or caress your face. The worst is when you are carrying someone in a stair-chair. This wonderfully medieval device is for carrying people up or down stairs. It is a fold up chair with two seatbelt style straps. One goes around your lap and the other across your chest. A wise paramedic will wrap a sheet around the patient to keep them from reaching out and grabbing things. This avoids being thrown off balance and injuring everyone involved.

Despite my best mummification efforts, certain patients have managed to get their hands free. This allows them to grab railings or worse, your face. Carrying the patient is a two-person job with one paramedic at the head and the other at the feet. The one at the head is the one at risk of having his or her face touched and is truly helpless to do anything to stop it. If you let go of the stair-chair, it will go crashing down on your partner. Tempting though this may be (depending on your partner), it gets you a pretty bad reputation.

Generally, I handle bad smells well, but occasionally, times arise when I have a pre-existing weak stomach due to flu, a hangover, or bad food at lunch. I ride a bike to work so I never bring my departmentally issued cooler with me and sometimes my food goes off. I tend to challenge my GI system and the consequences can be dire for all involved.

On New Year's Day we got a call to the Annex at 5:30 am for a diabetic lift assist. Someone had fallen out of bed and couldn't get back in again. No injuries, they just needed help getting into bed.

My partner is attending but I walk in the room first. She's lying on her side in bed and says, "Look at what I've done." Without thinking, I pull back the blanket to assess her and there is a massive, fully intact, firm-looking, fresh, dark pile of shit in bed with her. She said it just happened five minutes ago. If she rolled on her back she would be lying in it, but fortunately she has the strength to stay on her side.

When I pull back the blanket, I release a thick wave of poo-smell that had been concentrating and bonding into a dense noxious cloud. The smell hits me all at once. It's too fresh, too strong and attacks me by complete surprise. I start to gag. Puke is imminent. I run from the patient's room to the kitchen where I dry heave a few times. I regain my composure and re-enter the room to assess the patient. Right in the doorway the smell hits me again. It isn't as strong, but the smell/memory centre of my brain is overwhelmed. I run from the room to the kitchen but this time it all comes out. I'm retching and puking and filling this poor lady's kitchen sink with vomit. I have tears in my eyes. I can't do this call.

My partner is a hero. He comes out and says, "Stay here. I'll take care of it. This stays between us."

"Okay," I reply feebly. As I start cleaning her sink, he goes back in the room to change her bedding and clean her. She has home care coming at 9:00 am, which is just a few hours away, but she needs to be cleaned up now or be degraded and humiliated by resting in her own filth. A lot of people would have said, "Cleaning up shit isn't my job. Let the home care do it."

This was a night shift on New Year's Eve. We left our station the moment we booked on, and didn't return until 7:20 am the next day. We did 16 calls that night: drunk, stupid, violent, annoying calls. We were tired and stretched. My partner went above and beyond his job description to do the right thing and help this patient keep her dignity and not have to sleep in her own shit.

It's not all car crashes and heart attacks on this job. He is an example of a good paramedic and a good person.

Speaking of being a good person *or not*, I confess I threw up another time, on another call and I didn't clean it up. The one-room apartment was so disgusting with shit, piss, blood, puke and rotting food that I didn't think she'd notice if I left a sink full of vomit.

I'm not of proud of myself. It was a new personal low. I'm just telling it like it is.

The call was for a woman who fell and couldn't get up. It was called in by the person who delivers her meals-on-wheels lunches*.

We walk into the apartment and there is a strong smell of Code 5. We leave the bags in the hallway because there is nowhere to put them in the apartment without getting them contaminated by all the bodily fluids on the floor. The entire room is like a giant biohazard waste dump.

Even though we were told that she is alive, we half expect a corpse because of the strong Code 5 smell. Fortunately/unfortunately the patient is very much alive. She is lying on the ground glistening and gooey, covered with a sticky gelatinous slime that we are relieved to find out is honey. This honey is all over her face, arms and torso. She has a giant industrial sized tub of it and is eating it by the handful. She has essentially glued herself to the ground and, with the help of alcohol, can't get up.

There is feces and urine all over the floor because she hasn't been using the washroom. She says the blood is "mostly menstrual," but what finally pushes me over the edge is the stacks of rotting meals-on-wheels containers still full of food. It is very hot in the one-room apartment, the windows are all closed and the putrefying containers are bursting. I can't handle it and run to the kitchen to throw up in her sink. I obviously wasn't the first to use the sink for puke as I could see the layers of her previous visitors. I

* My last job, before I was a paramedic, was delivering meals-on-wheels downtown. I got fired for being a dangerous driver. The last straw (and most spectacular) was when I knocked over a street light downtown. They asked me what I was going to do next and they almost fell over when I said, "paramedic." They refused to write me a letter of recommendation.

figure, if anything, mine is a little fresher and, though it is hard to imagine, an improvement.

My partner and I are standing over her as we try to strategize how to get her out of her apartment without further contaminating ourselves. She interrupts our flow of thought.

"Have you seen my cats?" she asks.

"Your cats, ma'am?"

"Yes, I have four."

"How long has it been since you've seen them?"

"A month."

My partner and I look at each other. Code 5 smell mystery solved.

Why? How?

I had been working in theatre as an actor / director type since I was 17, but when my first son was born I decided that I needed something a little more *steady*. At the time, I was working as the Artistic Director at KYTES which is a drama program for street involved youth. One terrific aspect of the program was called Future Options, in which Leesa, the Future Options Coordinator, would research job interests for the youths involved. She would find out what schooling was required and what other skills or preparation were needed to apply for a certain job. She would also bring in someone who was currently working in the field to speak with the youth and help decide if it was something that he or she really wanted to pursue.

One of the youths wanted to become a paramedic. When Leesa talked about paramedics, it sounded really cool. I always liked things that were medical but never wanted to spend much time in school. She said that it was a one-year program at Centennial College, which seemed reasonable to me. I lived within a few blocks of a Centennial campus, so that seemed very convenient. I was about to be laid off for a year (a pattern I was not enjoying), so I figured it was the perfect time. I would start receiving EI (Employment Insurance, the dole, pogey) and go to school for a year to become a paramedic. After a year, I'd get my old job back again and then if/when I was laid off in the future I would have this backup paramedic career waiting for me. Also, compared to an actor's salary, I would make so much money as a paramedic that working only two days per week could support my artistic habit.

The plan was perfect except for a few hitches: first, I didn't finish high school and so I didn't have any of the pre-requisite sciences for admission. After a year at George

Brown night school, I applied to the program and I got in. Second hitch: the Centennial Campus near my place on Carlaw is a Communications campus. For paramedics, I had to go to a campus called Warden Woods in Scarborough... *Scarborough!* Not Beaches-Scarborough. Not Lick's-and-the-Fox-Scarborough, but actual Scarborough. Far Scarborough. Scary Scarborough. Scarberia-Scarborough. I lived in Toronto my whole life and never went East of Pape. Warden Woods is at St. Clair and Warden. You have to remember that the mega-city was still a new concept and that Scarborough used to be a separate city. It was far and I didn't have regular access to a car, but I was already committed to the idea so I decided to make the commute.· As it turns out, it only took 40 minutes to get there on my bike. Shocking, but it was actually closer to Broadview and Danforth than my old job at Dufferin and Bloor.

During the summer I got a letter informing me that "*due to new province wide restructuring*" the program had changed from a one-year program to a two-year program. I had only been laid off for one year so this hit me pretty hard. I would either have to abandon my previously-dream-artistic-director-job or drop out of school after one-year. The last and most challenging option was to resume my directing job, work during the day and ride out in the ambulance at night. This is what I eventually did. I worked 10am-5pm and then rode in the ambulance from 7pm to 5 am. I kept an air mattress and a sleeping bag in my office and would sleep on the floor for a few hours in the morning. It almost killed me.

· I later learned, as a paramedic, that St Clair and Warden is only the tip of the iceberg when it comes to Scarborough. It goes *a lot* farther north and east. Amazing, but true.

After I got hired as a paramedic, I found out that this city has no part-timers so I had to work full time, which was, again, not part of my plan.

Full time work with three young kids made it hard to have room for anything artistic, though I managed to squeeze in a book and a live show.

I wouldn't have applied at all if I had known that it was a two-year program in Scarborough (which used to be a different city) that would lead to a full time job. So I kind of got tricked, but in a good way.

My First Hanging

I'd been on the job for only a few days when we got a call for a hanging. I'm very nervous (which should be interpreted as shitting bricks). My partner knows it's my first hanging and my first dead person. He's a super nice guy who has been on the job for over 30 years and he assures me that he'll help me through it.

I'm obviously agitated as we drive there. He keeps saying, "The number one thing is to stay calm."

"Yeah, yeah. Calm," I say dismissively as I mumble through my protocols for a VSA.

"Deep breaths. I'm telling you, if you're too excited, you'll make mistakes."

"Yeah, yeah," I say, again not listening.

All I can think about is getting to this guy as fast as possible. I'm psyching myself up as we walk in. I'm repeating to myself over and over again, "I can do this. I'm a paramedic now. It's a hanging. I can do this. I'm a paramedic now. It's a hanging." I repeat this mantra to myself as we descend the stairs to the basement.

The patient is completely naked and hanging by the neck. T he rope is tied to some exposed pipes in the middle of the room. I try to run in, but my partner puts a hand on my chest and stops me. From the doorway, my partner looks at the patient and asks what I want to do.

"Get in there and help," I say like it's a no-brainer.

"Ok," he replies, moving his hand from my chest.

As I run in, my partner reminds me that this is a potential crime scene and we need to be careful to preserve the evidence. I barely hear him. Standing in the doorway, he tells me that the first thing we have to do is to confirm that he's dead.

"What's the best way to do it?" I ask.

"Well, you can take your stethoscope and listen for an apical pulse."

I walk towards the patient, terrified. It's my first dead body. I raise my stethy and place it directly on his chest to listen for heart sounds, but every time I push against his chest to hear, he swings away from me. He's hanging from the neck and swaying back and forth. As I continue pressing the stethy to his chest he swings around to my side. I'm chasing him in circles as he pendulums around me.

My partner continues watching from the doorway. The patient is spinning in circles every time I touch him, which makes me spin in circles like a dog chasing his own tail. The pressure is on and I need to solve this problem.

Finally, I put a hand on his back to keep him from spinning and I listen. I concentrate really hard and I hear a heart beat: a strong, steady, fast heartbeat. I'm about to yell out, "He's got a pulse!!!" when I think better of it and check my own pulse instead. With two fingers on my carotid and my stethy on the patient's chest I listen and feel. The pulses match.

I am so scared my heart pounding in my ears. I can't hear anything but my own pulse. It is so loud I'm sure everyone in the room can hear it. I'm near consumed by panic. How am I supposed to hear someone else's pulse when mine is so overwhelming? I suddenly realize that my *experienced* partner has stayed in the doorway this whole time. I think about this and figure that he probably would be helping me if he were worried about the patient. I realize that I must have missed a step. I take a deep breath and tell him, with sheepish insecurity that the patient has no pulse.

When I think back, I know my partner was teaching me a lesson. The patient was obviously Code 5, but I was tunnel visioning and forgot to check for signs of obvious death. He wanted to watch me squirm a little, so that I'd never forget. It worked. Though it was embarrassing, I understand and I've never forgotten. I'd do the same to a new guy if I had the chance. In fact, someday I hope to.

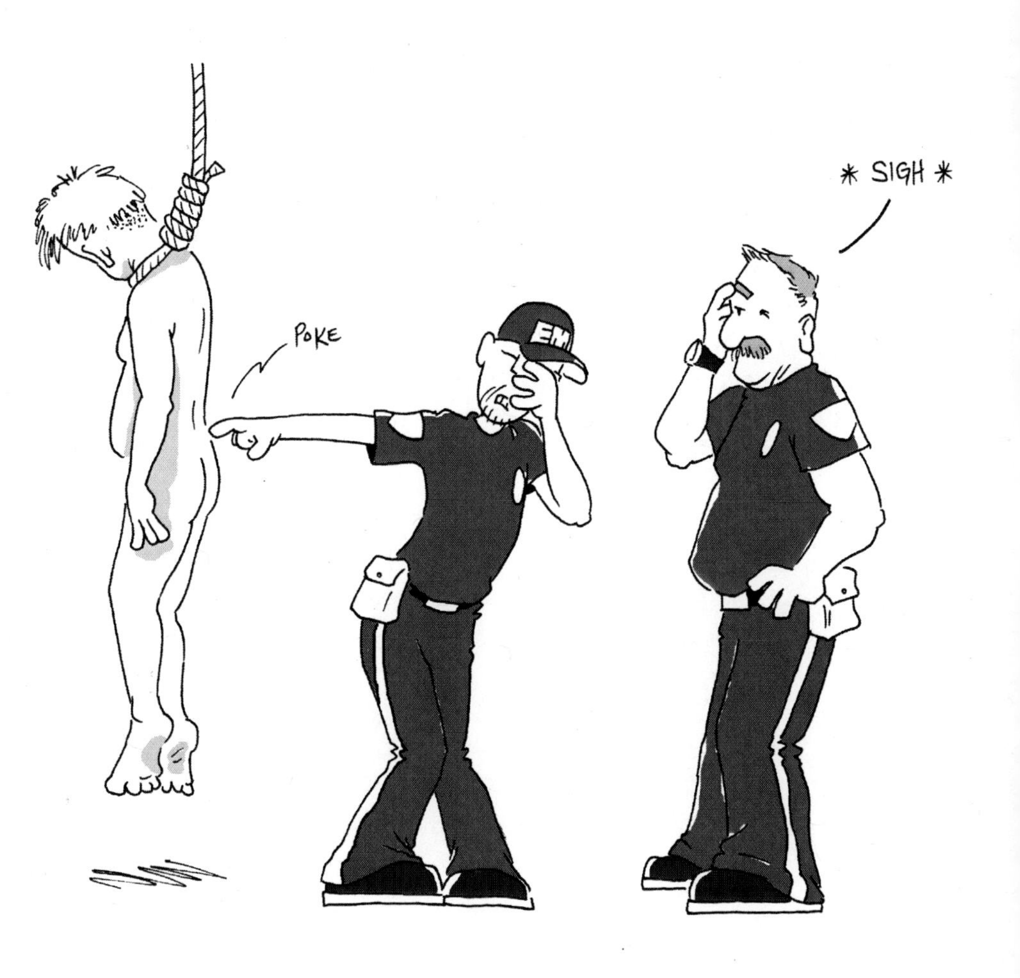

Naked SOB·

We get a call for a 36-year-old female who is short of breath at an address on a dodgy street in Scarborough. We enter and she is sitting on her couch, panting in the lotus position, completely naked. On the walls all around her are S&M gear and sex toys. Not classy upscale S&M gear, but the cheap and flimsy kind. If the Dollar Store had an adult erotica section, this would be it. I feel like I'm in the porn aisle of Zellers. There are vibrators, dildos, whips, ball-gag masks, lubes, beads, costumes and more. These are on hooks and displayed on shelves for showing off or for quick access. This isn't her dungeon; it's her living room. This is the first room from the front door. You know the porno where the plumber/pizza/delivery guy arrives at the house of the lonely housewife and is all wide-eyed and surprised by what he sees when he walks in the door? This could be the set and my partner and I are the plumber/pizza/delivery guys. Fortunately, if we had to vote, two out of three of us don't want to cue the funky bassline.

I've done more than a few difficulty-breathing calls in my time, so I can usually recognize the difference between an anxiety attack and an asthma attack from the doorway. This is clearly anxiety. I cancel fire before they can get out of their truck. I do this partly to prevent them from getting a name and claiming that they were the first to make patient contact and partly because I have a feeling that once they set foot in the room with this woman it will be hard to get them to leave.

I reach for a blanket on the couch and say, "Ma'am let's just get you covered up."

· Keep in mind that SOB stands for Short of Breath.

She waves the blanket away, "That's ok. I'm fine."

"I think it would be better if you were covered up." I wrap the blanket around her.

She removes the blanket. "Don't worry. I'm very comfortable with my body."

I wrap the blanket around her again. "I'm less comfortable with your body and I'd feel better if you were covered up."

Alcohol is my Job Security

Being a paramedic is one of a public figure· representing a medical service. In the public eye, I strive to be as professional and as respectable as possible. When someone calls 911, it is because they think there is an emergency. They don't have my experience, perspective, or perhaps, mental stability to discern a major emergency from a minor emergency or, as is more often the case, a minor annoyance.

I deal with a lot of stupid people and I try not to let them know my real thoughts. I'm there to help, not to judge; regardless of what kind of a doorknob I think they are.

"Oh yes sir, of course I believe you. You were at the Farmer's Market and you bought some fresh vegetables and after your shower you were walking around your condo naked and unknowingly sat on a carrot that hadn't been put away and was left on the couch. No, it makes perfect sense. It really does. Oh, there might have been two carrots? Well, we'll explain that at the hospital. Yes, I'm sure they'll believe you, too. It probably happens all the time. Vegetable related impalements happen more often than you'd think. You're okay to walk out to the ambulance, right?"

To the patient we are as respectful as possible, but as soon as they are out of earshot, we're all, "You should hear about the dumb-ass I just brought in."

· In early versions, I accidentally wrote, "Being a paramedic is one of a *pubic* figure..." This Freudian slip was not caught for the first three editions. It was tempting to leave it in as people either didn't notice, or or thought I was telling it like it is.

These are the tales of two alcohol-assisted patients who represent my bread and butter. You tell me which you think is more likely to win a Darwin Award one day.

Guy 1 is drunk and driving his car in Scarborough. He runs a red light in front of a police car. He sees the cop, the cop sees him, he sees that the cop sees him and he decides to make a break for it. He goes left through the red light and down a one-way street the wrong way. The cop flips the lights on and pursues him. He tries to lose the cop by driving down an alley. In the alley, he hits a pole so hard he wraps his front end around it. His head hits the windshield and breaks the glass, but he doesn't give up. He throws the car in reverse and, miraculously, it starts despite the front-end damage. He backs up and smashes into the police car. The police officer jumps out to arrest the man who he finds sitting, seat belted, in the driver's seat yelling, "I'm only the passenger, the driver ran away!!" over and over again. At Scarborough Gen. he is now handcuffed to the stretcher, on a backboard and sticking to his story about being the passenger. He's also yelling abusive obscenities to the police and everyone who walks by.

Guy 2 is the passenger in a pick-up truck that is driving through the city. He is also drunk and decides to hang out the window and give celebratory 'Whoo-hoos' to people on the street after his team won some significant sporting event. He is practically standing up outside the window of the truck and feeling pretty cool with the wind in his hair and everyone's attention, when the truck pulls around a corner. Wham! He gets hit in the head by one of those metal street signs that are posted along the road. You know the ones that say, "Don't hang out of cars, you dumb-ass."

Amazingly, it didn't tear his head from his neck. The top of his scalp, however, is de-gloved. It looks like someone wearing a yarmulke which fell off, or when the wind catches someone with a toupee and flips it backwards. The firefighters were especially impressed/disturbed when my partner asked them to hold the flap back so that he could directly palpate the skull for integrity. It was solid.

St. Mike's is the closest hospital so we decide to bring him there. St. Mike's is in a funny position as a hospital. They are the best hospital for a major trauma downtown. Any gunshot, major car accident or serious bad-ass trauma that happens south of Eglinton (the south half of the city) will go to St. Mike's. They are also a Stroke Centre and have a helicopter pad on the roof to bring traumas from all over Ontario. They handle the worst of the worst. On the other hand, they are right downtown and deal with most of the drunks from either the club district or from the many homeless shelters that are liberally peppered around the area. This means that they are over-worked, deal with a lot of bullshit and are not easily impressed.

On scene, our guy was unconscious. There are varying degrees of unconscious and most people don't qualify as truly unconscious. If they can be woken with a shake or a loud, "Hey, wake up!" then they're not unconscious. We refer to this as sleeping and we do not consider this to be a medical emergency. In fact, sleeping is quite therapeutic and should be encouraged. This guy can't be woken up and this is generally regarded as bad.

We called the hospital from the scene so that they would have an opportunity to assemble some staff. En route, he started waking up and by the time we got to the hospital he was talking and seemed lucid. Consequently, the nurse is giving me a hard time for treating the call so seriously.

I give the whole story about him lopping the top of his head off, but she only looks me in the eye, unimpressed, and says, "And?"

"I dunno, I kinda thought that was enough. Maybe he has high cholesterol…"

I'm trying to explain the situation, to make her understand the condition of the patient on scene, but she isn't listening. She only spins everything I say into downplaying the injury. She sends him to Major, which is still for sick people, but she does it reluctantly. I'm being met with nothing but disrespect until a nurse asks the patient where he is.

"I'm shingling."

"I don't understand." The nurses, my partner and I all look at each other, not knowing what he means.

"Shingling. What does it look like I'm doing? I'm shingling. I'm roofing. I'm putting on shingles."

"Where are you shingling?"

"On a house at Pape and Queen. Why can't you understand that?"

With that said, we got a bed.

In actuality, neither of these guys qualifies for a Darwin Award. Although stupid, they both still have the possibility to contribute to the gene pool.

I'm a fan of the drink as much as the next guy and a little more than some, but I can't help thinking that the world would be a better place without alcohol in it. About half my call volume is tied to alcohol in some way: violence, assaults, suicides, accidents, falls, MVCs, PIs. And then there are all the damaging health effects like cirrhosis of the liver and increased chance of a brain aneurism.

Don't get me wrong. I'm not saying to get rid of booze, because if we did, paramedics would be out of a job, not to mention a coping mechanism.

Cycling Shoulder Lady

Never assume the relationship of any two people on scene. I've said, "Your grandfather is going to be just fine." Only to have her reply that it is her husband. I've also had patients kissing passionately only to be told that they were brother and sister.

When I was a student we did a call for a woman in her 40's who had dislocated her shoulder while cycling in a park downtown. We arrive to see that she is being comforted by a man who obviously knows her. She tells us that they were cycling together when she fell and hurt herself. My preceptor starts asking about her medical history but she is being evasive. He really drills her about the importance of understanding her history in order to give her pain killers.

"Do I need to tell you now?" she asks.

"I can't give you any pain killers until I know pharmaceutically what you already take. Some drugs mix badly."

"Ok…" She takes a deep breath and begins, "Celexa, Clonazepam, Lorazepam, Diazipam, Prozac, Zoloft, Effexor, Wellbutrin, Thorazine, Haldol, Zyprexa, Seroquel, Risperdal, Lithium, Tegretol, Ritalin, Valium, Librium, Antabuse…"

She goes on and on naming all these different psych meds: antidepressants, anti-psychotics, mood stabilizers, anti-anxiety pills and everything under the sun for every mental disorder known to (and created by) the pharmaceutical industry. When we package her up to leave, I turn to the guy who had been comforting her and ask if he is coming to the hospital.

"No," he replies. He then turns to the patient. "Well, it was nice meeting you," and walks off.

My preceptor looks at me and then asks our patient what her relationship was to the man.

"That was our first date."

What's the Worst Thing You've Ever Seen?

Sometimes at a party, when someone finds out I'm a paramedic, they'll ask, "What's the worst thing you've ever seen?" Paramedics often get asked this question and we hate it. Other people within earshot will usually become quiet because they've been secretly wondering the same thing and a bizarre hush will fall over the crowd.

People who ask this don't fully appreciate the gravity of this question: paramedics don't just see things on the job, we experience them. When you drive past a car accident and you see something terrible, just remember that we had to climb into the car with them.

I've had people die in front of me. People to whom I had just been speaking, and then my voice was the last one they heard on Earth. When they die in the back of the ambulance, it is often just me and the patient, alone. It isn't the same as "seeing" someone die. On television you see people die all the time and it usually doesn't keep you up at night.

What they are really asking is "What's the worst experience of your life?" I don't see other people getting asked this at parties. But it happens to paramedics all the time. I don't know what people expect me to say...

"The worst thing I've ever seen? Well, it was probably a call for a 15-month-old baby. She had been playing in the front yard with her parents, just crawling around.

At one point there was a mix up between the parents about who was going to stay watching her. The Mom went inside the house and the Dad went to his car. They each thought the other was taking care of their daughter. The baby crawled into the driveway and the Dad, not knowing the baby was there, accidentally backed over her head in the family car. Her head was crushed under the rear wheel and she was killed instantly.

We could have pronounced her dead on scene, because she was, after all, code 5. But she was a baby and for a baby, you want to give every chance possible. You can't just look at the parents and say, "I'm sorry." You have to do something, even if you know it is impossible that the outcome will change. The police set up a run and we drove faster than we ever have before, but she was declared dead at the hospital. Knowing that she wasn't going to live didn't make it any easier when the doctor said to stop CPR.

The family agreed to donate the baby's organs for transplant. I understand that the organs of a healthy baby are incredibly valuable and I understand that many babies lived because of getting those organs, but for the paramedics, it meant that we had to intubate, do CPR and breathe for a headless baby all the way to Sick Kids."

Is that the story they were expecting? I know it isn't, and that is why we never tell it, but being asked makes us remember it one more time.

I guarantee that if you have ever asked a paramedic what is the worst thing that he or she has ever seen, you will not have heard the true answer. They'll tell you the worst thing that they don't mind talking about, but the worst thing they've ever seen is reserved for a therapist or an unfortunate bartender.

The Worst Thing I've Ever Seen (That I'll tell at a Party)

When I'm at a party and I get asked, "What's the worst thing you've ever seen?" I have a set answer. "If there is one thing I've learned from my job, it's that paper cuts are the worst..." Another is, "Well, there was this one time that I was walking into the locker room just as my partner was getting out of the shower."

Paramedics love to tell gory stories at parties. It makes the experience worthwhile to get some entertainment value out of it later. There is a formula that applies to this situation, which I first heard from Woody Allen, though due to the "democratic" nature of the internet, figures including Mark Twain, Carol Burnett, Lenny Bruce and (my favourite, though least likely) Marie Osmond have all been credited with saying:

Comedy = Tragedy + Time.

Unfortunately, sometimes paramedics lose perspective on what is the normal human experience regarding death and gore. More than a few times, I've been at a party and told a story that I thought was pretty funny and when I get to the end the person listening to the story is just staring at me, not laughing, just shocked. And I'm like, "Don't you get it? She was already dead before I got there." And they will say something like, "So she died alone and no one missed her?" And then I feel like I should be all professional and dignified and it kills the story.

So, you want to hear the worst thing I've ever seen? It's ok. Everyone does. That's why people slow down as they drive past an accident. The most gruesome thing I've ever seen (not counting people who have been dead a while, those people have their own category for gross) was a guy who was hit by a subway.

We got a Delta for "a body at track level." They never say, "hit by a train." They say, "contacted by a train", "personal injury at track level" or, this time, "body at track level." When you describe it like that, it sounds like the patient died of natural causes and magically appeared under the train.

We arrive and, of course, there are a million people on Yonge St. waiting for the shuttle buses. I can hear people bitching about the TTC (Toronto's public transit) and how unreliable it is. It always surprises me how much people complain about being inconvenienced by the subway not running after a person has been *killed* by one. I find it difficult to sympathize with someone who thinks their day is hard because they will be late for work when someone else found that day so hard that he offed himself. I want to say, "Oh, you're upset by the delay. How upset? Put your money where your mouth is and prove it. The subway will be running again soon and I expect to find you at track level."

I suppose they don't know, or believe, that someone has died, or maybe they just don't care. I'll tell you this, which was told to me by a TTC body-clean-up guy: "Nothing stops the subway from running except a jumper. If you are on the subway and they tell you to exit for some reason, mechanical or otherwise, then the truth is someone got hit by a train."

I do plenty of calls to the subway for sick people. It may cause a brief delay, but they *never* ask you to get a shuttle bus unless someone dies. Most people would be surprised at how many jumpers there are: almost one a week. They rarely make the news so as not to influence other suicidal people to try the same technique. I've always been surprised that suicidal people are so easily swayed by the power of suggestion. You'd think we could get them to do something more productive.

We arrive to find all the TTC staff halfway down the tunnel. As we walk in, the fire fighters are leaving. One says, "Not much for you to do, unless you have a shovel."

The body is between the tracks in a most unnatural shape. His head is missing but we know that he is male because his pants were torn off and are around his knees. Both his legs are broken in so many places that they bend at several impossible angles. He looks unreal, like a Halloween decoration. It looks like someone stuffed a plaid shirt and a pair of pants with straw and threw them on the ground. His green spring jacket is torn to shreds and his torso is folded backwards like a Swiss Army Knife. His abdomen is open and disemboweled. I can identify many, if not most, of his internal organs. Surprisingly, there is very little blood. If it were a horror movie, you'd say it looked fake and low budget.

My partner goes through the deceased's pockets to look for ID. It's one of those situations where if we were watching a movie, you would think the actors were crazy to approach the body. You'd be yelling at the screen, "Get out of the subway! Don't you know you're in a horror movie!!" I stand beside my partner, just in case we actually *are* in a horror movie and the body grabs him. Though I don't know what I'd do. Hopefully, I'd be the guy about who you say, "Ah, man. They killed Morgan. I liked that guy."

As we walk up the tunnel there are bits of the patient streaked down the track. Fifty feet up the tunnel is most of his head. The skull is open and his brain is in pieces in front of it. He appears to be either face down (literally) or his face is elsewhere. It is absolutely gruesome, but I'm fascinated by the anatomy. I missed *Body Worlds*, that dead-body-corpse-art-show at the Science Centre. Seeing our patient is just like that, except fresher and with the need to worry about getting bits of the display on my shoe.

It's an amazing opportunity to examine human anatomy, but I don't want to show how morbidly interested I am in front of all the other emergency and TTC workers. I want to get as close as possible, but I don't want to look like a psycho or worse: a keener. One also has to be very careful because it is a potential crime scene and you can't contaminate evidence.

The police take photos and measurements of the whole thing until they can rule out homicide. Then the TTC body-clean-up guys come to dispose of the corpse. There is an unmarked door at the end of every subway platform that leads to a refrigerated room. The purpose of this room is to store the body until nighttime when it can be taken out more discretely. The TTC clean-up guys can tell stories that put mine to shame. They must be really fun at parties. Those guys should have their own show.

No longer gasping

We got a call to a nursing home. The pager says, "Delta short of breath. 89-year-old female. Difficulty breathing, patient gasping." We are driving lights and sirens when we get an update, "Call downgraded to a Charlie. Patient no longer gasping." Charlie is a lower priority, which means we can use our discretion about using the lights or not. We decide to continue driving lights and sirens because... well, it's fun.

As we walk past the nursing station, a staff member, who doesn't make eye contact and continues shuffling papers, says, "We couldn't get a blood pressure." This doesn't surprise me in the least. If you have regular dealings with nursing home staff, then you know why·. Even if they had provided me with a pressure, I wouldn't have trusted it in a critical situation, so I'm not too phased.

When we arrive, we find that the reason she is no longer gasping is because she's dead. This also explains their difficulty in getting a pressure; as does it confirm any sweeping generalizations I might make about nursing homes.

We begin to work her, but in classic nursing home reality there are no staff at her bedside to give us patient information and no one has even noticed she died. They just noticed that she wasn't so noisy anymore.

· In earlier editions, I was more blunt and said that most nursing home staff were incompetent. I had someone get mad at me for making this statement, saying that his wife was a nurse in a nursing home. I said, "So ask her. If she's in a nursing home, she *knows* most of them are incompetent and if she can't tell..." This didn't go over well. I'm not saying what he did for a living, but let's just say that he wore a white shirt to work. I'm more mellow now and self-edited to be kinder and more respectful to nursing home staff. See, I listen when I'm talked to.

Euthanasia

Working in this job I see a lot of people in the last few years of their life. Nursing home calls. The call info will say something like 'Female, 96, decreased LOA'. That's Level Of Awareness and basically indicates how conscious or aware of their surroundings they are. This can be a very relative thing. Some extremely elderly people (like both my Grandmothers, 95 and 100 years old) are sharp as a tack and help me with my crossword puzzles during offload delay, while other, younger people, are catatonic and haven't done more than stare in many years.

I went to a nursing home call a while ago for an elderly woman with a decreased LOA. We were met by an extremely distraught son who, when we asked what was wrong with his mother, just repeated, "Look at her!! For God's sake, just look at her!" This is not very helpful to us. I explained how I didn't know his mother and I wasn't familiar with what she was normally like. This offended him causing him to repeat his mantra of, "Would you just look at her?"

Let me describe your classic nursing home call: We walk into the patient's room at the nursing home, or rehab centre (that's for rehabilitative injuries, mostly hips, not drug rehab) with four people to a room; all of them are unconscious. Our job is to figure out which patient is the decreased LOA who we were called for. It is impossible to guess because none of these people can speak. We have to find a staff member to tell us why this unconscious person is more unconscious than they were last week and why this unconscious person is more of a concern than any of the other unconscious people in the room.

Amazingly, the staff will always be new to that floor, usually on their first day, and unfamiliar with the patient. Someone called 911, but that person is unavailable and everyone denies making the decision. Often, the explanation for a 911 call is that the nursing home doctor did his rounds and felt the patient should be taken into hospital and seen by a doctor. This amuses me. Generally the nursing home doctor is long gone to the links by the time we get there, but on occasion they are still around. They don't appreciate the irony when you say, "so you want her seen by a doctor? And your job is…" If I actually get to meet the doctor and I'm feeling grumpy, I'll say, "So you want the patient seen by a *real* doctor." I guess nursing home doctors went to medical school too, but it seems like a pretty sweet gig. As far as I can tell, the job goes something like this:

The doctor is doing his or her rounds and comes across a patient who says, "Doctor, I don't feel well."

The doctor replies, "You should go to the hospital. Nurse, call 911. Next!"

Now I know that if you had done a survey when these elderly patients were young, about how they wanted to spend their last few years on this earth, they wouldn't have chosen to be catatonic and strapped to a wheel chair flashing the "O" or the "Q" for the world. The "O" is where you permanently have your mouth in a fish guppy position. The "Q" is similar but with a tongue sticking out.

My parents are aging and my dad has already asked me to kill him if he starts getting Alzheimer's·. I don't think I can kill my dad, so I understand that it's hard to let go, but there are forgotten people in these homes. Some don't ever get visits. I have heard, too many times, a staff member say, "As soon as the kids get the money, you don't see them any more."

· My Dad denies asking this of me, which probably only furthers his concern about Alzheimer's.

If the family is emotionally unable to let go and they aren't visiting, then it is just selfishness. In nursing homes, I would introduce a one-year policy: if no one visits you for one year and you are catatonic, I say pillow therapy is in order. If the person has family or loved ones that visit and keeping the person in this vegetative state is helpful for their grieving process then by all means keep them alive, but if not, let them go toward the light.

Related insert (which wouldn't fit as a footnote): I just saw the film, *The Diving Bell and the Butterfly* and it changed me and the way I work regarding the perception of people who appear catatonic. It is the true story of a man who was on top of the world when he had a massive stroke that left him cognitively perfect but physically paralyzed, except for his left eye. He did all his communicating by blinking his way through the alphabet with that eye. He had a contract with a publisher for an autobiography prior to the stroke and honoured that contract by dictating his life story one letter at a time. The film is incredible. The book, on which the film is based, and which I plan to read, is also supposed to be phenomenal.

Back to my book, which seems kind of shallow to me now…

I'm not going to get into the moral, ethical, or legal aspects of euthanasia, but I am organizing a "kill me club" among paramedics, nurses and anyone else who is interested. Basically, everyone signs up and agrees to check in on each other as we get older. The more spry ones promise to kill the more feeble ones as time goes on. Now I appreciate that everyone has a different idea of when to go, so people get to decide their own criteria for being killed.

After all, we are talking about murder. For many it is the O or the Q, but I'm open to suggestions.

I know that euthanasia is illegal in Canada, but I'm also thinking about creating a voluntary activity program for seniors. I would call it Extreme Sports for Seniors: sky diving, rock climbing, scuba diving, jungle and desert trekking, race car driving, swimming with sharks –you get the idea. The waivers would be very detailed. I'm guessing the turnover on membership would be high. There would be no fees; that isn't what this is about. People would die with dignity while having fun. They could will the videos to their next of kin who would make a fortune on the Internet.

Broken Arm at the Bike Store

In the summer of 2007, my family and I did a road trip in a 29-foot RV all the way to Whitehorse, Yukon. It was awesome; a whole other book. Unfortunately, absentmindedness being my strongest characteristic, I lost all of my bike tools somewhere along the voyage.

I'm an avid cyclist and I like to do most of my own repairs. That summer, post expedition, a few things needed re-tuning on my bike and I still hadn't replaced my missing equipment. There are no tools in any ambulance station because, if there were, they would just be stolen. Hence, my bike was being neglected.

Halfway through the shift one day, we got a call to a bike store for a 40 year-old male who was test riding a bike when he fell and broke his arm. I think, "Oh boy, maybe he will cancel because it's not really broken and I can go shopping." Turns out, it really is broken and I'm disappointed at missing my chance to restock.

I'm attending and I'm working with someone who is new, so he needs a bit of guidance. I'm telling him, in rapid fire, what we need and what to do: "Get me a quick splint, a roll of cling, one pressure dressing, a triangular and a set of vitals." Then I turn to the bike store guy who is watching and say with equal conviction, 'I'm also going to need a set of Allen keys – good ones."

He gets a slightly panicked look in his eyes like I've given him a great task of extreme responsibility, "Allen keys, no problem." He runs off with determination. He comes back having replaced the panicked look with curiosity. "What are the Allen keys for?"

"My bike," I answer, offering money. "The seat's a little wobbly".

Bashing in a door

There is a saying that I use in paramedicine, which I adapted from carpentry, 'Check address twice, bash down door once.'

Often people call 911 and we arrive to find the door locked with no one to open it. Either they can't come to the door because of the injury or there is a mix-up with the address and we're at the wrong house. There have been some tragic results with the merging of municipalities to form the mega-city. Due to the existence of multiple streets with the same name it has happened where emergency services go to the wrong address. For this reason we don't break a door down without legitimate confirmation of the address and a serious concern for the safety of the patient.

We will do everything we can to not damage property, but we will if we need to. If we want to bash in a door for a medical emergency, we ask the fire department to do it·. We also have to call the police and it's a good idea to have a sergeant present. Assembling all these people can take some time. However, if we can see the patient and have reasonable evidence that a life is at stake, we can do it ourselves. Though we have no tools and I prefer not to bash myself into things. It should fervently be noted that just because someone called 911, doesn't automatically mean a life is at stake. If you haven't picked up on that from my book so far, I haven't done my job very well.

· You can imagine how much they love doing this. Who wouldn't love to destroy stuff under the guise of saving a life? It's a pretty cool perk to the job.

We got a call to a rather nice apartment building for a woman who is short of breath. We arrive, but can't get in because the door is locked. We can hear her screaming, so we know she isn't *that* short of breath, but we still don't know what's wrong. She just keeps screaming, "Help me. Please help me." We ask her to come to the door, but she keeps screaming, "I can't. Please help me, quickly." She won't say what's wrong and she won't stop screaming and I know I should be very concerned, but frankly, I find it a little annoying.

Friends of mine once had a similar call, but the door was unlocked and their story ended with a twist. When they opened the door (without police being present) they saw that the reason the patient was screaming and couldn't open the door herself was that she had been hacked apart with a machete. To add zest to the story, the guy who did it was still in the apartment. The point is, we take these calls seriously and you never know what is on the other side of a door.

We tried to call a superintendent to open the door, but he wasn't available. Her desperate and relentless screams for help cause me to believe that she must be in serious distress. Because it was a shortness of breath call the firefighters are there, so I tell the captain that we'll need to take the door down. He smiles confidently and picks up his radio to call for assistance.

One of the older cops on scene scoffs at the idea of needing the fire department to take a door down. "Let me show you how it's done." He backs up and pounds a powerful kick into the door. The door doesn't even shake. It's a steel door with a reinforced steel frame and clearly stronger than they were in his day. He is visibly jarred and stares briefly into the door. We are all silent. He turns and makes a great effort not to show the pain in his body or the limp in his step as he walks down the hallway without eye contact. None of us says a word, after all, he carries a gun. We never see him again.

Ten minutes later three beefy, calendar-posing fire guys show up. They are all wearing matching sleeveless grey beaters (which makes me wonder if they get them issued) to show off their hulking muscles, and each is carrying some object of destruction. One has a long handled sledgehammer, another has a weighted battering ram and the third has the classic long handled giant axe. Put blue face paint and kilts on them and they'd be ready to fight the British. I have to admit that they did look intimidating, except for the helmets, which are only useful if someone is spraying you from behind with a hose.

Before they're unleashed on the door, the captain knocks one last time and then as an after thought gained from a bad experience, he tries turning the knob to see if it has been unlocked the whole time. It hasn't been, but we don't question the wisdom of such a move. "Go get her, boys," he says. They take to that door like a starving man to a pizza. They pound, smash and chop that door until it finally falls open. It took longer than you might think. I was tired from just watching. The code standard for some of these apartment buildings is pretty hardcore; as I mentioned earlier – steel on steel.

Inside we find the biggest woman I have ever seen who could still more or less walk. She is leaning on a sofa chair, but not sitting in it. She is a perfect square with little feet sticking out. She is like a living 'Little Miss' character who is as wide and as deep as she is tall, but with corners.

I ask her what's wrong and she tells me that she has to go to the bathroom, but can't walk without her walker, which has fallen a few feet away. She can't bend over to pick it up because the shift in her centre of gravity would cause her to topple over. She didn't want to sit in the chair because her size/strength ratio forbids her to be able to get back out again, so she has been standing – needing to pee – for quite some time. She finally called 911 for assistance.

She's upset about her door being destroyed but refuses to leave it unlocked or leave a key with a neighbour since she's too afraid of being robbed.

She can't fit on our stretcher and we couldn't possibly lift her even if she could, so I'm very relieved to find out that this will only be a courtesy call.

After helping her to the bathroom, I say, as a confirmation that we won't be transporting, "What can I do for you *in your apartment*, now that we're here?" She wants to go to bed and asks if we can get her on to her left side. She has always wanted to sleep that way but can't physically get there on her own.

After a long struggle, we get her into bed and onto her left side. We then leave thinking, "there but by the grace of God, go I."

VSA, Can I help you?

We get a call to a VSA (Vital Signs Absent, or dead guy) in a home. We arrive to a big house in a fancy neighbourhood and the house is dark. I double check the address because this is unusual. Usually in a VSA, all the lights are on and someone is standing in the front yard screaming, 'Hurry, hurry' instead of doing CPR; this house, however, is all dark and quiet. My partner and I walk up to the house and knock on the door. A nervous looking 50 year-old man opens the door a crack and says, "Yes. Can I help you?"

"We received a 911 call from this address," I reply. "Does anyone require an ambulance?"

"No," he answers.

"Is it possible that someone else called 911?"

"No. It's just me and my wife here…" he says. I'm about to call dispatch to see if there was an error with the address, because there are several triplicate addresses due to the megacity thing, when he finishes his sentence. "…and my mother, but she's already dead." There is an extended pause while I process this statement.

"Is your mother in the house?"

"Yes. She's just inside, but there's nothing you can do for her."

"Can I see your mother please?"

He looks at me confused, swings the door open wide and says, "Sure, but I'm telling you, she's already dead."

I wonder if I should wait for the police first, because it is all very sketchy. Fire, police and another ambulance should be on their way. Our own ambulance is parked outside as a beacon, and I decide that there will be lots of people to help look for our bodies. Thus, with backup coming soon, I figure I'll walk into the house. Inside a 50 year-old woman, who is holding a baby, is standing in the hallway.

"What are they doing here?" she asks.

"They want to see Mom," he replies.

"But she's already dead," she answers calmly.

Now I am *really* wondering if I should be in this house. I finger the 10-2000 panic button on the portable radio, which would automatically send a distress signal to all ambulances and police. It interrupts all air communication and transmits 20 seconds of my microphone without having to push the button again and without making any sound. This is the time in an emergency when I would say, "Okay sir. Put down the gun. I won't try to escape. Just stay calm and stay standing by the second floor, front room, south-facing window with a clear shot from across the street and let's talk about this." The only hitch is that I can't remember if the 10-2000 button is the orange one or the purple one. I make a mental note to ask someone, if I survive.

"Can I see your mother, please?" I ask again.

"Sure. I don't see why though. She's dead. She's in the basement..."

Not the basement. *Anywhere* but the basement. Why the basement? I picture false walls and gimp suits as he points to a door leading to a potential dungeon. I curse my macho pride as I descend the stairs while listening for the rattle of chains.

"Leave the door open, please. The police have already been called and are on their way." I mention this ever so casually as a reminder both to them and myself. I debate telling him that I have high cholesterol and haven't bathed recently.

In the basement we find a very elderly woman on a bed covered with a sheet. She is dead with her hands folded across her chest. The bed is made and the sheets are tucked neatly around her. There is no sign of a struggle and judging by the set up in the room and the objects around, it looks like she was in palliative care. She's dead but is still warm. Technically we should try to bring her back, as she is newly dead, even though it is in no one's best interest to do such a thing. The man explains that she has been ill with cancer and just died peacefully this evening.

"Then why did you call 911?" I ask.

As it turns out, they didn't call 911. They called the funeral home to tell them that she had died. The funeral home called the police, because that is what you do when you have a dead person in your home, and the police called us by mistake.

In an expected death we do things a little differently. We confirm death and comfort the family more than we try to save the patient. Never underestimate the living as being the real patients in these calls. In my first three years, I received three complimentary letters from the public (and only one complaint, which isn't a bad ratio). The first two positive letters were from family members of patients who were Code 5.

Heroes

In 2006, the Royal Canadian Mint created the Medal of Bravery quarter to pay tribute to everyday Canadians who risk their lives to save or protect others. They don't specify, but we interpreted it to pay tribute to the emergency services: police, fire, ambulance.

The quarter is nice, but I chose this job. I went to school to learn the skills to do my job and now I do it. I don't think there is anything heroic in that. If I book off and don't come to work because I'm sick, or one of my children has a spring concert, someone else will fill my spot. They will do whatever I would have done that day. There is nothing unique about me compared to any other paramedic. When you call 911 and I show up, it could have been anyone. Theoretically, we all know what we're doing. I believe that a hero is someone who does something special –something exceptional, something above and beyond what is expected of them.

When a pilot lands a plane successfully, nobody calls him a hero. He's just doing his job. Lives are at stake and he saved every one of them, but he doesn't get his picture in the paper at the end of every flight·. Or when an architect designs a bridge that doesn't collapse, she isn't called a hero. Or when a chef caters a wedding for 400 people and nobody dies from food poisoning; that person was just doing his or her job. It is expected of all of them that they do their job well and people stay alive.

More people are killed or injured on construction sites than in the line of duty for all emergency services combined. Construction workers don't get a quarter

---

· Although I like that for flights to Cuba, the passengers always break into applause upon landing. It's a nice gesture.

dedicated to them. No one calls them heroes for risking their lives to give us housing or buildings or bridges. I know how risky their work is: I'm the one who takes them to the hospital.

Certainly, we, in emergency services, deal with more unpredictable situations than many jobs, but I don't feel anyone should knowingly risk their lives any more than people doing any other job. We have training, we have equipment and we have back-up plans. That said, there have been amazing acts of heroism from police, fire and ambulance; people who have gone above and beyond what is expected of them. Sometimes, it gets publicly recognized, more often it doesn't. So even though it is nice, I don't believe in calling *all* emergency workers heroes all the time. That is just my opinion. Some unnamed members of the allied emergency services who wear red suspenders feel differently. They milk the hero thing.

Police, Fire and Ambulance

"Why do you have to be with that doctor? You should find yourself a nice firefighter to settle down with."

-A post 9/11 cartoon of a mother talking to her daughter.

"Eat 'till you're tired, and sleep 'till you're hungry."

-The life of a firefighter, as told to me by one.

Police, Fire and Ambulance. It's no coincidence that you always hear them referred to in that order. Usually, you just hear people mention police and fire when talking about the emergency services and we are forgotten entirely. Listen for it, you'll see. It's like looking for a white pickup truck. Once you start being aware of it, you see it everywhere.

Firefighters, police and paramedics are all like cousins in a family business who get paid and treated differently. Paramedics are the adopted red-headed step-children who get all the chores that their brothers and sisters won't do. We're the youngest, so no matter how old we get, we're still the baby of the family –and treated as such. It's hard to believe, but we aren't even considered an essential service.

Police and ambulance get along fine. Before I was a medic, I worked with street youth and people with mental illnesses. To say that I had a different perspective on issues of police powers would be a huge understatement. I came into the job with the anti-police sentiments that are common for anyone who works with people who are regularly on the receiving end of the nightstick. My opinion regarding police has improved after getting to know some of them and working alongside them. Police have a crappy job and deal with crappy crappiness all day long.

We ask for the 10-200's (our fancy word for police·) all the time. Sometimes, we ask for them because the call is more of a police matter (like an assault with no injuries) and sometimes because of a concern for our own safety. I know that if I'm ever in danger on the job and I call in a 10-2000, the police will come very quickly. 10-2000 means that a paramedic's life is in danger and they take that very seriously.

I knew a medic who was downtown dealing with a patient who suddenly became violent. They tried to control the patient, but he was cracked out and too strong. The patient began to get the better of them. One managed to run to the truck and call in a 10-2000 while the first medic continued wrestling with the guy. As soon as the 10-2000 was called, this seemingly homeless man jumped into the mix and helped subdue the guy. He was undercover and was watching the whole thing. The medic asked the undercover cop how long he was going to let him fight with the patient before stepping in. "I dunno," the cop replied. You were doing okay,"

Cops also know that if they get hurt, we'll put a rush on it for them. We actually count on each other personally and regularly enough that we get to know each other, and that makes a difference.

Fire is different. I think the only people who dislike fire more than ambulance is police. They call them 'the evidence destroyers' or 'the basement savers'.

· We call them "the twos" for short. I think this term comes from their non-emergency phone number, which in Toronto is 416-808-2222, but I'm only guessing. Seems like a lot of 2s to be a coincidence.

The relationship between the fire department and EMS is much like Americans and Canadians. Fire has to always be number one. They want everyone to notice them all the time. They drive lights and sirens to most calls, even if it isn't an emergency, just to make their presence known.

Fire has a wonderful relationship with the media. Their media relations department is well organized, well established, well staffed and thus a well oiled machine. They even have their own photographers who make sure the papers always have a flashy photo for their cover. Fire never misses an opportunity to be in the news to herald what they are doing. Part of this is practical: EMS is bound by patient confidentiality and can't disclose any information to the media about a patient. There is no confidentiality about property, so fire can talk all they want and as often as they want. It also helps that fire gets to hang around on scene doing interviews when we have to leave and take the patient to the hospital.

If you want to know why EMS feels bitter, you should visit a fire hall. It'll have a workout room, wide screen TV, satellite, DVD player, barbeque, beds·, fresh renovations and a stockpile of food. Ambulance stations have TVs, but if we want cable, a medic has to sign up for it in his or her name and get everyone to chip in for it. If there is a DVD player it is because a medic donated it. We don't have beds because the assumption is that we won't be sleeping, we'll be out working –which we are.

Basically, fire chiefs are really smart. They saw the writing on the wall when buildings became safer and fires happened less often; they started getting into prevention, awareness, public safety and public relations. Fire gets paid to go door-to-door checking on smoke alarms. We could

---

· I really could have just stopped at beds.

have a similar program where we go door to door and ask people if they have any tripping hazards on their stairs, if their medicine is properly labeled or other safety issues around the house. It would be a great way to provide work for people on light duties or to give medics a break when they need off the road and to not deal with patient care.

If EMS were smarter, or as assertive as fire, we'd find the money from the city for prevention or to grow in some way, but we don't. We cut corners instead of demanding for more budget money. In 2011, Toronto's mayor Rob Ford, who is most likely the worst, dumbest and most dangerous mayor that North America has ever seen, said that all city jobs had to be cut by 10% across the board. He said this with no research all. Just a general idea that there is too much "gravy" and that everyone should lose 10%. We just laughed, because we don't have 10% to lose. We've been cutting for years while police and fire have been growing. The KPMG report actually said that fire's budget is too high and our budget is too low. His own report said that we are understaffed and underfunded, but we are still expected to cut 10%.

The fire department line is, "If we don't get more money, babies will burn in their beds." Who resuscitates those babies? We do.

A few years ago we actually laid-off a bunch of medics at the end of their probation. We didn't have the funds to keep them past the summer. Management said they would hire them back the next year, but by then, most of them had already taken work with another service.

Around the same time someone in our management said that we should reuse blankets from patient to patient if they weren't *visibly* soiled, as a cost cutting measure to save on laundry. Can germs live on blankets? I don't know; ask the First Nations people what they think?

Fire is smart, powerful and organized. The Red Mafia doesn't get pushed around. They protect their own, and power to them that they do. In 2006 when that fire truck got stolen from outside a Home Depot while the guys were shopping; they tried to stonewall the police. The police wanted to investigate and, at first, the fire chiefs wouldn't cooperate. Fire said they wanted to handle it internally. This was a criminal act involving the theft of city property valued at over $300 000, but they didn't want to cooperate with the police. If an ambulance were stolen while we were shopping, we'd be hung out to dry by management. We'd be fired and martyred for the whole city to see. No protection at all.

Every year at my kids' school Spring Fun Fair you see a full firefighting crew with a fire truck for the kids to climb around on. I asked the organizers why there is never an ambulance. "We asked, but they couldn't spare one," is the answer.

The explanation that fire does so much work that isn't directly related to firefighting is because they are overstaffed and are being paid anyway so we might as well find work for them to do (hence all the public relation gigs). The argument for fire being so overstaffed is that fire needs the extra bodies in case of a disaster[*], but the same logic isn't applied to EMS. We always function at minimum car count. Doesn't anyone think that someone might get hurt during these disasters that require so many firefighters? A disaster isn't just a subway or plane crash (both have happened here since I came on). I did a call where two mini-vans full of children collided at high speed. One vehicle rolled over. Twelve patients, nine of them were children. We had to transport two of them together, because otherwise, there wouldn't have been enough ambulances. One patient was a 6-year-old girl with an open fracture to her femur and the other had possible internal damage from the seatbelt. Twelve patients required almost half the ambulances in the South East. And that was only one accident that doesn't even qualify as a disaster. Meanwhile, there are still all the regular 911 calls that continue to happen and need to be taken care of.

The public would be outraged to know the amount of times I've been the only ambulance in the South East. The only ambulance available to service one quarter of the city – a city with a population of 4.5 million. This is a danger to the public not to mention embarrassing for the service.

---

[*] I would like to take this opportunity to apologize to my family in Southern California who can regularly see smoke working its way over the mountain towards their home and often need to brush the ash off their lawn furniture. Those firefighters have a very different reality than the firefighters where I live and I mean no disrespect to them and others that see working fires regularly.

We need more ambulances and more paramedics on the road. On any New Year's Eve there will easily be a waiting list of 20 people who have called 911 and will be waiting a long time for an ambulance because we have none to send. So what do we do? We send in the fire department as first response.

Fifty percent of fire calls are medical calls. They even put that in their advertising flyer –they have an advertising budget to hire more firefighters when it is unbelievably competitive to get hired in the first place. For ninety percent of those medical calls, we cancel fire the moment we walk in the room. When the ambulances are all busy, we'll send fire to do first response on low priority calls. They'll stand around the patient and do the Circle-of-Healing until we arrive and break up their Stare-of-Life so that we can send them back to the station for a nap. Why do we use them for medical calls? Why? They aren't medically trained. It isn't their fault, it just isn't their job. Granted, sometimes we do need them for backup: lifting heavy patients, holding a head still, CPR or other basic skills. I think it would make sense to have the portion of their budget used for medical calls to hire more medical people. That way we would have actual medics for back up. Is it a crazy thought to call another medic to help a medic do a medic's job?

People have said to me after reading this, "Wow, I had no idea there was such a rivalry between fire and EMS." There isn't a rivalry between us. We each have a job to do and we each do it well; it's just that the public perception is that they can do our job. Let me say clearly and definitively: they can't. No matter what they think their first-aid certificate qualifies them for. I've read in the paper many times about firefighters taking someone to the hospital or giving pain medication: Both of which they can't do. Besides, when there is such an extreme power imbalance, you can't call it a rivalry. It would be like saying Italy and Nepal have a rivalry at the World Cup. Or the USA and Peru have a rivalry to declare the leader of the free world. It is only a rivalry if the dominant party chooses to care and engage. I doubt most Fire are even aware of any bitterness with us or Police. It's sort of the opposite of Carly Simon's "*You're so Vain (you probably think this song is about you)*", it's more "*You're so Clueless (you don't even know we wrote a song about you).*"

Every once in a while there is an inter-emergency service competition; usually it is a fundraiser or as an excuse to party out of town. We, as EMS, don't take them too seriously, because, as I said, we are tremendously outnumbered and rarely come out on top, but occasionally we get our moment of glory.

A few years back there was a fundraiser for a Jane/Finch youth organization. They invited Police, Fire and Ambulance and challenged everyone in a bicycle race around the Jane and Finch neighbourhood, which is one of the rougher ones in the city (the EMS station out there is called The Knife and Gun Club). Of course, most of the competitors were Police and Fire with very few medics (actually, I think there was only one, but I don't want to be charged with exaggerating the drama of the story). I love a good underdog-come-from-behind story as much as anyone and probably more than most[α], but this one is a touch better because it comes with some snappy Hollywood dialogue.

[α] Ask me sometime about my daughter's grade 2 cross-country race. The greatest running story *ever* and I'm a bit of a connoisseur of running stories (Note the Gallipoli reference coming up.).

As you've already predicted, our lone medic-representation won the race, but my favorite part is this little exchange of dialogue from after the race.

Cop – I saw you before the race, I didn't think you'd be so fast.
Medic – I saw you too. I thought *were* going to be fast. I guess we were both wrong.

Oooh. Snap.

I sound bitter and I am, and I acknowledge that it is mostly jealousy. Fire has a job to do and they do it well. I wouldn't want anyone but them putting out a fire at my house. But present day doesn't reflect the history that established their powerful situation. Houses have fire codes and better wiring. In the past, fires have devastated entire cities, but that doesn't happen anymore[·]. Medics on the other hand, used to be ambulance drivers with no more medical skill than a present day firefighter. Now, however, we run IVs, intubate and can administer more than 30 kinds of life-saving drugs. In the 50s we just drove people to the hospital. Now we *are* mini mobile hospitals.

Another key element to bear in mind is that insurance companies insist and lobby for fire stations to be evenly distributed and close to every home. Of course they do; why not use public money to reduce insurance payouts by private companies. The public should rise up and insist that ambulances stations be distributed the same. After all, it is your health and life at stake. But, alas, home insurance

---

[·] Yes, yes, perhaps it doesn't happen because there are so darn many firefighters. Fine. If we had more ambulances, maybe nobody would ever die anymore either.

is privately run and a for-profit business, while health insurance isn't. When corporations risk losing money, they don't mess around. Especially, if they can spend government money to boost their profits.

Some municipalities have amalgamated fire with EMS. Personally, I wouldn't mind their political clout, but something I learned from the Australians in Gallipoli is to never let another country be in your command.

Interestingly, it is always fire that complains about merging stations with EMS. I find their complaints laughable, but it gives you an insight into our respective jobs, responsibilities and workloads. They complain that we don't do our share of chores (cooking, cleaning, shopping, etc.) in the station. This is because we are mostly out of the station doing calls. They also complain that we wake them up at night with all of our coming and going, which we like to call *working*.

A few stations here are shared, but they are still run as separate services under one roof. The first time I was at a certain station, which is shared with Fire, I was greeted by a firefighter. He approached me with a smile and asked if it was my first time in the station and would I like a tour. I thought this was very friendly, so I agreed.

"This is the kitchen. We have separate sinks. Don't use our sink. The TV is ours, don't change the channel. The fridge on the left is ours, don't take any food. The fridge on the right is yours; there might be some mustard in it. The food in the cupboards is ours, don't touch it. This door leads to our bedrooms. Don't go in there. You don't have a bedroom. That door goes to our crew room. Our crew room has the big screen TV and a gym. Don't go in there. Your crew room is in there. I heard your TV is broken. Fire eats in the kitchen and you guys eat in your crew room."

That was my experience. I have some attractive female medic friends who had a very different experience and were made to feel very welcome by fire. They were invited to join them for dinner and encouraged to share the TV. I can't imagine what the difference was.

I want to be clear that I have nothing against the people who do the job. Most firefighters I've met have been great guys; especially ones that I've met off the job. Firefighters are just like paramedics, police or anybody. In any broad collection of people, you'll have extremes that will tarnish the images of most. I've never met one off the job who I didn't like.

I purposely chose not to tell any stories of firefighters being less than useful on calls, because Lord knows I've been less than useful on a few calls too (and it is actually my job)·. Besides, it isn't fair to judge them on

· I especially decided not to tell any stories about firefighters endangering the patient and making the situation worse, because I don't want them kicking my ass.

their performance during medical calls; they aren't trained medically, regardless of what they feel is the value of their First-Aid training.

If a firefighter wants to write a story critical of the ambulance folk, I encourage it (after all, they've got time). It would be educational to hear their perspective and might create dialogue and help with communication. I honestly don't know what they'd complain about though. They might write something like this:

So we did a call for a 35 year-old woman who was short of breath. Her medical history was anxiety and fibromyalgia so we were pretty worried about her. When the paramedics arrived, I stopped them in the doorway so that I could tell them what we already learned; like the patient's name. The paramedics wanted to walk past me to see the patient, but I wanted to tell them about the medications first; after all, I had spent a long time copying them down one letter at a time.

"Is the patient on fire?" he asked.

"No," I replied.

"Then get out of my way."

That really hurt my feelings. He was mean.

If I could be a firefighter, I'd probably do it, it's a pretty sweet gig after all, but I'm too lazy to change·. Also, I like being a medic. There is nobility to being the underdog or the lowest rung on the ladder. You always

· The real reason I don't switch careers is that I wear glasses. If it wasn't for these cursed specs and my fear of medical intervention, I'd be gone-daddy-gone to a fire hall faster than you can say, "Is it my turn to marinate the ribs?"

have something to complain about, and you're justified in doing so. A good indication of the sweeter gig is that there are lots of people who have left EMS for Fire, but NO ONE has ever gone the other way.

When I was first hired we had a three-week orientation and many people came to speak to us. There were 21 people in my hire, a pretty rag-tag bunch. We weren't used to starting work at seven o'clock in the morning and everyone was brain dead from sitting in a classroom. One day a big-wig fire-guy came to speak to us about working together on the road. He strutted in and stood at attention in the front of the room. We stared back at him. Half of us had our heads on the table. We looked as bored as we felt.

He scanned his audience; time was measured in drops of spittle hitting the table. In a mixture of confusion and disappointment he said, "When I walk into a room of new-recruit firefighters, they all stand at attention."

"Guess I picked the right job," was my reply.

Enough ranting. I know that all these feelings would go away if only someone dressed up as me for Halloween or had ambulances on their pajamas.

Things I won't even bother to bring up:

-Firefighter calendars.

-*They* call themselves *Lifesavers*.

-They call their trucks *Rescue vehicles*.

-Dalmatians (I know they don't really have station dogs anymore, but the fact that they ever did makes me jealous.)

-Fireman poles (so cool).

-Firefighter calendars.

-24 hour shifts mean that they work 7 days per month.

-Apartment buildings have lock boxes at the front entrance containing a key to open the front door if the patient is unable to buzz you in. Firefighters are the only ones to hold the key to the lock box.

-The biggest elevator always has a picture of a firefighter's helmet.

-*Every* firefighter has a second job. I guess even they feel like they should work for a living.

-Firefighter calendars.

-Firefighters have food drives where the public can bring food donations to a firehall. We do this too, but it never works out because we are never in station long enough to receive them.

-Firefighters get hired first and then get paid for training. Unlike us, who pay for school and then look for a job.

-The World Police and Fire Games also invites customs and corrections officers and… Hmmm, it feels like someone else should be there too... I guess not.

-Firefighter calendars.

-Firefighter calendars.

-Firefighter calendars.

Girl with Her Leg Caught in Her Bicycle

We get a Bravo to a residential street in Scarborough for a 5-year-old girl with her leg caught in a bicycle. While pedaling she managed to get her leg caught between the frame and the pedal arm. Unfortunately, she has a coaster bike so the pedal doesn't turn backwards and her leg is in the way so it won't go forwards.

I'm bending down trying to assess the leg to make sure it has circulation. She is shrieking like only a five-year-old girl can and my head is at her mouth level, making it especially piercing.

Judging by the relentless screaming and continuous blows to my head every time I touch her leg, I conclude that she is in a tremendous amount of pain and that it might actually be broken. The leg is really jammed in there, but her inability to hold still and stop screaming make it very difficult to asses. It appears to be losing circulation and I can't get it free. I can't transport her with a bike attached (the emerge really doesn't appreciate when you do this), so with a heavy heart, I call for the fire department to bring the jaws of life and cut the bike in half.

As I make the call, a neighbour says, "Cycle Solutions (appropriately named) is just around the corner. Should I call them?"

"Yes," I reply. "Explain the situation and get them to send someone over."

As soon as he hangs up the phone, I see a guy come running, around the corner carrying a toolbox. Upon arrival, he pulls out a few wrenches, takes apart the bottom bracket, pulls the pedal off and releases the girl in less than a minute.

Fortunately, nothing was broken and the blood quickly rushes back into her foot. She immediately runs over to her mother and the guy puts the bike together again. Good as new.

As he is reassembling the bike, a fire truck comes around the corner with the sirens blaring. I give them the satisfactory wave of "No problem. Keep driving. Go back to your barbeque and satellite TV."

The girl was fine and didn't need to be transported to the hospital. That bike-guy was the real hero. He used his skills outside of his job description to do a great thing. I nominated him for an EMS Community Service Award and he won. They created a plaque for him and there was a ceremony at headquarters.

I wasn't invited or even told about it, but, hopefully, he was.

Pregnant Lady/Speaking in Tongues

We get a call for a woman, 38 weeks pregnant, in labour with her 4th child. This is important information because babies deliver quicker the more children the mother has had. I'm pretty nervous. I've never delivered a baby, although I was more or less present for all of mine, so I get the general concept. It's one of those things that, as long as there are no complications, it is pretty easy (for the paramedic). Mom's really deserve all the credit for delivering babies, but they are usually too exhausted from the ordeal to high-five anyone.

Did I say I was nervous? Freaking out would be a more appropriate description.

As we enter the apartment, I note that there is a lot of African art on the walls. Two women come to the door dressed in African clothing and they are speaking a language to each other that I don't understand. I ask if they speak English, but they don't. I ask what language they do speak so that I can try and get a telephone translator through AT &T. She says a language that I've never heard of.

You should know that I love languages, and I pride myself on knowing a minimal amount of several; just enough to make me functionally useless in all of them. I have no idea what language she just named. Then she says dismissively, as if it were impossible that I could speak something so obscure. "Est-ce que tu parles français?"

"Oui!!" I respond with much enthusiasm and gusto.

Now, me saying I speak French so confidently is definitely an overstatement. I'm not going to say that I'm a complete stranger to the language of love: after all, I took grade 11 French three times, but I should have been a little more humble about it.

She immediately starts speaking to me in French and an amazing thing happens: I respond, appropriately no less. I am suddenly lifted out of my body and replaced by Gerard Depardieu, except that I don't feel the urge to urinate in the aisles of airplanes after I've been drinking. I am speaking French at an impossible rate, using vocabulary that is impossible for me to be familiar with. I am speaking in tongues. I'm asking about her due date, the health of her pregnancy, the results of her last ultrasound, if the child is head down or breach, if her previous deliveries had complications, if she has an OBGYN, what hospital she is scheduled to deliver in. These are subjects that I am very sure were never covered in any of the years I did grade 11 French. I am pretty sure that I would have remembered a conversation between Roc LeRock and Brigitte LaBombe, if it had been about birthing scenarios. I not only ask her all these questions, but I can understand her answers perfectly. I am possessed.

There is a quiet moment during transport where I reflect on the call and feel very proud of myself and my French. It is during this quiet reflection that I realize that I can't possibly speak as well as I have so far. There is a brief moment of lucidity where I realize that I'm not myself and that I am doing the impossible. It's like when Wile E. Coyote finally notices that he has stepped off the cliff and is standing in mid-air. His awareness of having no solid ground beneath his feet causes him to suddenly fall.

I panic with the realization that I've stepped off the cliff and have no solid ground beneath me. I fall and I lose the French completely. I can no longer put simple sentences together. Every failing test from every year of grade 11 French is flashing before my eyes. The panic is growing at the thought of needing to deliver this baby with a language barrier. I'm aphasic. I feel like I've been cursed on the Tower of Babel. I now can no longer speak any language, including English.

I take a deep breath and utter a prayer to the soul of Gilles Vigneault. A trancelike state washes over me. I picture myself in a black and white striped shirt with a beret and a thin moustache. In my mind I have a baguette under one arm and a bottle of red wine under the other as I ride my bicycle, with a wire basket containing a small dog that I don't pick up after, along the riverside. My love for mime and Jerry Lewis grows inside me. I mumble a few words of Gens de Pays and suddenly, I am back in. I'm fluent again. At this point, I could work for the UN. It's bizarre. I probably sold my soul to the Separatists.

We get her to the hospital, without delivering, and drop her off. I do some last translating for the hospital and then leave feeling proud of myself. When the call is over I turn to my partner and I look at him as if for the first time. "Pierre," I say as if he has just appeared before me. "You speak French. You should have done this call."

"I was going to offer, but I couldn't get a word in edgewise."

My Other 'Almost' Delivery

The closest I've ever been to delivering a baby was when I arrived a few minutes after a woman, who was alone, gave birth to a baby girl in her kitchen, coincidentally, on my birthday.

Mom was sitting on the kitchen floor holding the baby with the cord still intact. The tiles felt cold and she was surely uncomfortable. She said she was in the kitchen, because it was the only room in the house without a carpet.

The baby was crying, pink and vigorously moving so I felt pretty confident that it was a healthy delivery without complications. I dried the baby, cut the cord and showed off my swaddling expertise. It was pretty special; it being my birthday and all. The mother only spoke Spanish and Cantonese so my parental chit-chat was minimal. I thought Spanish might have come miraculously to me under the circumstances, but it didn't. Perhaps I wasn't panicked enough.

If I had started speaking Cantonese, it would have been a miracle of biblical proportions. I would have looked closely at the placenta for outlines of Mary. It would have been worthy of a Shyamalan film. The only Chinese words I know are swear words left over from my Chinese friends in elementary school. Without ever practicing these words they have stuck in my lexicon of profanities. Of course, this isn't the proper venue to show off my very limited Chinese vocabulary of explicatives, so it was mostly a lot of smiling. If I had been there 10 minutes earlier for the actual delivery, I probably would have had a good review of cursing in Chinese.

We struggled through communicating until the midwife, who spoke Spanish, arrived. I suggested naming the baby Morgan, but she wanted a Chinese name.

Delivering Babies

This is a little update for the 2013 edition, because about a month ago, I delivered my first baby. I could have edited the previous story, but once you start re-writing history, it's a slippery slope. Next thing you know wars have different winners and I was taller with a six-pack. So, I decided to add this little chapter.

In early 2013, I earned my first stork-pin· for delivering a baby with my new partner, which is a lovely way to start a new partnership. Well, I shouldn't say that I delivered him, I really didn't do a thing; I was driving the ambulance. Actually, I was barely even driving the ambulance. It all happened so fast.

After loading Mom up, I put it in drive, moved about 10 metres and heard my partner yelling for me to stop driving. I put it in park and heard him yell, "there's a baby back here." I walked around to the back and opened the doors to give him a hand, but he appeared like an octopus with eight arms doing different tasks in different directions at the same time. I could only stare at the speed and accuracy of all his limbs.

I suggested the name "Jon-Morgan", but again, the parents had already chosen one.

This is the only time that I have been present for the miracle of birth for a baby whose last name wasn't Phillips (though I have arrived moments late and cut a few cords). I, myself, have a quarter-dozen children at home and have been present for all of their births, but I didn't remember it

---

· The stork-pin was discontinued as part of cut-backs deemed as gravy, so when I say "stork-pin", it is only an expression and shouldn't be confused with an actual pin that I might wear and be proud of.

being so messy. When you don't have to clean it up yourself, it isn't the same.

I attribute delivering one baby in ten years to the fact that, during a pregnancy call, I move really fast. I don't bother with silly things like a medical history or vitals, I just ask which hospital Mom is scheduled to go to, and if it makes sense, we get rolling there. You may say, "Morgan, you're an ambulance, not a taxi service. You should do a proper assessment. What if the patient has pre-eclampsia and has dangerously high blood pressure? You wouldn't know."

You know what is worse than not knowing your patient has high blood pressure? Finding out they have high blood pressure and not being in a hospital.

Don't worry Mom (my Mom), I'm not negligent, I do everything important: I get vitals and a complete history, but I do it en-route, thank you very much. I had someone with less years than me say, "you've never delivered a baby? I've been on for six years and I've delivered eight."

"Then you move too fucking slow," was my only reply.

Jail Calls

We do calls in jails, or court holding cells all the time. Sometimes, people have a legitimate medical concern, but usually, it is an attempt to delay the inevitable. Generally, inmates who ask for an ambulance have just been sentenced or are about to be transferred from a small holding cell to a big scary jail. I suppose it'll count as time served and just about every nurse will be cuter than your next potential bunkmate so, though annoying and a waste of services, I understand wanting to go to the hospital. If I were arrested, I won't deny that I may develop a severe allergy to handcuffs and drinking from a tin cup. We call it "incarceritis."

Jails are so surreal, at least they are if you're not wearing a shirt with a number on it. For the inmates, I'm sure it feels very real.

The first time I did a call in a jail, I felt like I was in a prison-breakout movie. As we went through every security check-point, I pretended we had a tiny Asian acrobat hiding in the airway bag who was going to leap out and help set free my wrongly-incarcerated brother. I had a giddy silly smile on my face the whole way up as I imagined the scenario.

The whole procedure went without incident. Prisoners are always very cooperative, after all, they are getting a vacation from jail and don't want to screw it up. We picked up the patient, handcuffed him to the stretcher and proceeded to leave. On our way out, I had the same feeling that I was in a breakout movie, except that now it was reversed. The patient was still going to escape, except that in this new scenario, I wasn't in on it. I imagined a white panel van pulling up, shooting me, hijacking the ambulance and taking the patient away to a country without extradition privileges.

My imagination was getting away from me and it was much less fun now that I was going to get shot. The whole walk down the long ramp to the ambulance, I tried to memorize the license plate of every van that drove near us. Of course, we got to the ambulance without any Hollywood twist.

One thing I learned is to never ask why the patient was arrested. You may think it is an issue of confidentiality or bias, and you would be right. Confidentiality isn't so much the concern, but the bias it creates can be hard to overcome. This call was a transfer from The Don Jail to Toronto Gen. It was simple and straight forward; he wasn't sick, it was just a transfer. He was just being brought to the hospital to have some tests done. No assessments or anything. I was feeling bored so I decided to read his file.

Turns out he was arrested for putting ads in the paper for modeling opportunities. He'd have young girls meet him in hotel rooms under the guise that he would photograph them and make them famous, instead he'd sexually assault them. I felt sick being near him. He was handcuffed to the stretcher and I just wanted to beat him with a D-tank. Funny, I don't think the term paramedic-brutality exists.

Off Duty

Q "How do you know who the firefighter is at a barbecue?"
A "He'll tell you."

One big difference between firefighters and paramedics is that firefighters wear their t-shirts off the job. They want people to know they are firefighters. Paramedics never do that, because we don't want to be asked medical questions when we're off the job. Firefighters are less worried that someone will spontaneously combust and then require their services.

We generally prefer to avoid getting involved in what is perceived as an "emergency". This may sound harsh and uncaring, but the reality is that very few people who call for an ambulance need one. Most people only need a ride to a walk-in clinic at best. If there is a real emergency, of course, any self-respecting medic will step in, but *real* emergencies are actually few and far between. The most critical part of our job is deciding how emergent the emergency. This needs to be determined quickly and we're good at it. It is perhaps our greatest skill and only comes with experience.

The problem for off duty medics is that when someone hurts himself and you, in plain clothes, state authoritatively, "Nah, he's ok," the general public thinks you're a bastard. Especially when you tell them that you're a paramedic because they wouldn't take your advice as a regular person. Then they get mad at you for wanting to leave and not sticking around for the ambulance that you know will take a long time because it will get dispatched as a very low priority.

When I'm off duty and watch the news I think, "Man, I'm glad I didn't get that call." Every paramedic has a different reaction when they hear an ambulance and they're off duty. Most don't hear it at all. They turn off that frequency in their brains. Others hate it like fingernails on the black board. Me, I love it. If I'm off duty and I'm out walking around or with my kids and I hear an ambulance, I think, "Not my problem. Somebody else is going off to get puked on, not me."

Hot Calls/Bad Calls

I'm not an adrenalin junkie. I don't pride myself on the amount of blood I've seen. I don't get off on other people's trauma or being on the news and I don't think I'm an anomaly among medics. It's like any large group of people; you have extremes that stand out, but most of us are pretty normal.

There are several different categories for types of calls. These include, but are not limited to: Easy, Bullshit, Brutal (in a sense of annoying or boring, as in brutal for us), Hot and Bad. The first 10 minutes of the TV news, or the front cover of the newspaper, these are all either Hot Calls or Bad Calls. Hot Calls are different from Bad Calls although they may seem similar, and on different days the same call may mean something entirely different; there is an element of subjectivity. Let me explain:

Hot Calls are fun, exciting and challenging. These are the ones that got you into the job; the ones that get put into TV shows; the ones you tell at parties (or one-person-shows). In this context, a brutal murder is very interesting. You get to pretend you're on CSI and try to figure it out.

We did a call to a factory in the late fall where a boss had been beaten to death in the furnace room. You could follow the story by the trail of blood. You could see where he tried to hide under the stairs and was dragged out. You could see a spray of blood for every time he was hit. We arrived before the police. He was Code 5 (early rigor) so we didn't touch anything (other than move one stiff arm) in order to preserve the evidence.

When the employee, who found the body, was asked by the police if he had any enemies, the employee stated "Many guys were angry with him that he wouldn't turn on the heat."

He was *dead* in the *furnace room*. Maybe it's a sign that I've been doing this job too long, but I find that funny. These murders are fine for me. Long since dead, no big deal, no emotional attachment.

Bad Calls are different. Bad calls are no fun at all. You talk less about Bad Calls. These are kid calls, domestic assaults, sexual assaults, and calls which are a little too familiar to something from your own life.

These are the calls we get paid for. These are the ones they warn you about in school. These mean stress leave, or counseling. These are the ones you can't stop thinking about when you want to fall asleep. These are the ones you don't tell your spouse about when you get home. These are the ones where you and your partner drive back to the station in silence.

It isn't what you see that haunts you. It's the decisions you make and the weight of responsibility afterward. It's hoping that you didn't make a mistake, but knowing that you might have. It's the second guessing and wondering what you should have done and promising that you'll do it different the next time; even though that situation will probably never come up again. We're always one shift away from needing to make a phone call to our staff psychiatrist or the Peer Support Unit.

The Penis Guy

This is for Brad Hart who inspired me to do this show, and consequently this book, by saying, "I'd pay $5 to hear the Penis Guy story again."

I am getting Chinese food at Dundas and Spadina during a night shift when my pager goes off for a Bravo hemorrhage. A Bravo is a medium-low priority. Don't tell anyone, but depending on the Bravo, I wait until my food is ready. After about a minute the pager goes off with more information: "*Male 42, feeling bored, cut off own penis and flushed down toilet*."

My first thought is, 'I hope my dinner is ready, because (not that I'm hungry anymore) I have to go now.' I rush out to the truck and see my partner sitting casually behind the wheel. I ask if he has read the page, "Yeah. Bravo hemorrhage."

"Did you read the details?"

"No, I just saw it was a Bravo."

"MALE 42, FEELING BORED, CUT OFF OWN PENIS AND FLUSHED IT DOWN TOILET!!"

After a stunned moment he reacts in a way that I didn't expect. He starts pounding the steering wheel with his fist and yelling. "Why? Why? Why? Why do I get all the penis calls?·"

Now I didn't know this at the time, but it was his first day back from stress leave after a bad call. He and

· After a show at the Cameron House, a medic from the audience came up to me and told me that he had worked with the same partner after this event. They had gotten a call for a "*male, 79, bleeding from the penis*". The partner reacted the same way and started hitting the steering wheel in the same fashion. Shortly afterwards, we began referring to his truck as the '*unit*-unit'.

another partner had gotten a call for a male acting strangely in an alley. They went in with police and saw the gentleman in question. As they approached the guy, they could hear him saying, “the aliens are coming to get me. The aliens are coming to get me.

“Sure Buddy,” my partner said to him. “Come into the ambulance and we’ll talk about it.”

“No, you don’t understand. They can read my thoughts. I’ve got to get rid of the transmitter.” Suddenly he pulls down his sweat pants, grabs one of his nuts and slices open his scrotum with a broken light bulb. The testicle falls out and rolls onto the ground – still attached to him. The medic, his partner and the cop jump on him, subdue him, roll the testicle back up, and take him to the hospital.

This is my partner’s first day back. This is the call to get him back in the saddle, so to speak.

So we’re racing, lights and sirens, through the city to get to this guy. Normally we wouldn’t run a Bravo·, but I hope that if my penis is ever cut off, by accident or otherwise, that the responding crew gets there as fast as humanly possible.

· I would like to note that an *amputated penis* was designated as a Bravo. Clearly, a female call-taker.

As we're zooming along we get an update on the pager, "*Patient will meet you at Eddie's House of Ribs on Shuter*." I was not expecting this.

We begin discussing the logistics of doing an amputated penis call in a rib house when we get another page. It says, "*Patient has been instructed to stay in his residence and NOT to go to Eddie's House of Ribs.*" We agree that this is some good advice.

We continue blazing through the city like only a couple of guys can when they're on a mission to save another guy's junk.

We drive past Eddie's House of Ribs and arrive at the patient's residence near the dubious intersection of Church and Shuter. As we're pulling out the stretcher, an irate man comes down the street yelling at us. We ignore him, because hearing a man ranting incoherently in this neighbourhood is really not unusual enough to get our attention. As he gets closer we can hear more clearly what he is ranting about.

"What the hell do you think you're doing? This is a quiet street. Making so much noise. I got neighbours. I told you to meet me at Eddie's House of Ribs!" Those last few words stop me in my tracks like a splash of cold water.

"Sir," I ask. "Did you call 911?"

"Yeah, but I wanted you to meet me at Eddie's House of Ribs. You think I want all my neighbours knowing my business?"

"Did you harm yourself this evening?"

"Yeah, I cut off my penis!"

"Where is the penis now?"

"I flushed it down the toilet."

"Is it still in the toilet?"

"No. I made sure it flushed down. Now my wife will never come back to me."

"I don't doubt it."

We get him into the ambulance so that I can assess him with some privacy. He is wearing black jeans that glisten and appear wet. He is standing up and when he unzips his pants, I see that his tighty-whities are also wet and bright crimson. He has a few socks rolled up into balls and stuffed into his underwear to soak the blood. I ask him to remove them. One by one, he slowly and calmly removes the socks and drops them onto the floor of the ambulance. They each land with a sickening thud/splat. He pulls down his underwear and his pubic hair is so thickly matted with congealed blood that it is hard for me to see what's what. Pardon the pun, but I can't make heads or tails of it. I can't even tell where the end of his penis is. I ask him to show me and he reaches down lifting a stumpy nub in the centre of all the blood and hair. When he lifts this nub, a spray of bright red blood shoots across the ambulance and hits the back doors.

"Putitbackdownputitbackdownputitbackdown!" I shriek with my voice cracking. I quickly hand him a pressure dressing and instruct him to hold it there while I set up the stretcher. We start driving to the hospital and my partner sends the hospital an update so that they can be prepared for an amputation.

He makes himself comfortable on the stretcher and I start asking him the usual questions about his past medical history.

"Have you ever had any heart problems?"

"No."

"Breathing problems, like asthma?"

"No."

"High/low blood pressure, diabetes, seizure?"

"No."

I prepare my pen for the next question and ask, "Psychiatric or mental illness?"

"I get depressed, sometimes."

"Are you taking any medication for it?"

"I used to take Paxil."

"Maybe you should start taking it again."

There is a reality TV show filming for one of the cable channels about the emergency room and as we arrive with the patient there is a camera crew running to meet the ambulance.

"We heard you have a trauma coming in. Can we film you?"

"I don't think this would be appropriate for the show."

"Why not?"

"You're going to have to trust me on this one."

"Is it something personal?"

"Mmmm, yeah."

As we bring him in, all the security guards are standing, looking with great interest and big shit eating grins as we wheel past them. "Is this the guy? The one that..." they ask cryptically with various gestures below the belt. I nod, continue past them and wheel the patient into a bed in Major.

We put him onto a hospital bed without incident and wait a moment for the nurses to arrive. Other than being mad at me for not meeting him at Eddie's House of Ribs, he has been completely calm, quiet, cooperative and in no distress. That is until the nurses arrive and put in an IV, then he yells, "OW! That hurts. What are you doing to me? That hurts more than when I... You know. Ow, that hurts."

We can only stare.

There are two nurses in the room, a male and a female. The female nurse has another question:

"What did you use to cut it off with?·"

"A Mach 3 razor."

The male nurse turns to him, "Mach 3. That's a good razor."

The patient says quietly, "It's a <u>very</u> good razor."

· That question did occur to me before we arrived at the hospital and I was going to ask him, but a part of me thought, 'Who cares what he used? IT'S GONE!!" Now I see that it would have been worth asking and I made a note to myself that the next time a patient chooses to sever his relationship with his manliness, I'll ask.

Please, Not On My Stretcher

We picked up a patient who was drunk in the club district. No injuries, just so drunk that he couldn't walk and other club goers were worried about him. When they aren't hitting each other with bottles or pushing each other down flights of stairs, there is a really supportive sense of community among trendy clubbers; that is until you look at someone's girlfriend. It warms the heart to know that people are looking out for you, even if it is only to watch the effects of the rohypnol that was slipped into your drink.

Our patient is in his 30s, well dressed, hair cut short and styled with a strong (perhaps overpowering is a better word) cologne. He is outside the club, facedown in a small pool of vomit. I asked the group of people who were standing around if any of them were his friends. None were. Then he vomited again and it occurred to me that, more likely, none were willing to admit knowing him.

We packaged him up and went to the hospital without incident. Like many drunk people, he had been sleeping the whole time; blissfully unaware of the spectacle he has made of himself as he lies on my stretcher.

As an obvious drunk with no other complicating factors, he becomes a low priority at the hospital, so we are on offload delay. Time goes by, and as the hospital predicted (which is why they don't give us a bed), he slowly starts to sober up. We watch his head bob around and move in laboured circles. Slowly, he reaches for his wallet and removes it from his pants pocket. He also removes his keys, some change, a few streetcar tickets, some random notes on pieces of paper and a lighter. He is slow and methodic about doing this and he has our complete attention. His determined movements are upstaging everything in the emerge right now. We are fascinated and completely absorbed.

Once he has completely removed everything from his pockets he rests these objects on his stomach. With cupped hands, he holds them in place, takes a deep breath and lets his head slump to the side in relaxation. We only had a few seconds to wonder what the whole production was about because urine started to flow over the side of the stretcher and onto the floor. FML.

Assault in Crescent Town

We go to a call for a "15-year-old male assaulted". It happened in front of his apartment building, which is part of a large complex of apartment buildings in the East end. Like most tightly assembled apartment complexes, it is generally populated with immigrants and people with lower incomes. This building in particular has a lot of refugee families from Afghanistan. We arrive in the patient's apartment where he explains that he was beaten by a large group of youth who were waiting for him and his younger brother. The gang surrounded our patient as he was leaving his building. They yelled racial slurs and hit him repeatedly.

The sparse apartment barely has any furniture; a few Arabic scriptures and some middle-eastern art adorn the walls. It appears that they've just arrived in Canada and didn't bring much with them. The two-bedroom apartment is full of women and children: the mother, grandmother, aunts and several kids, but not a father. The line that stands out, for me, from The Kite Runner is, "*Afghanistan is a country robbed of fathers*." The patient's younger brother keeps yelling, "He's hurt. He's lying when he says he isn't. He's hurt."

Between the residents there is a lot of heated discussion in another language regarding the boy being attacked. Although I don't speak the Dari, it's clear what they're saying. I gently assess the boy: bruised with nothing broken, minor bleeding. The mother is, understandably, extremely emotional. She's crying. I want to reassure her, so I tell her that her son will be okay.

"No he won't," she says. "No he won't be okay."

I try to explain that the injuries are only superficial and that although it will hurt tomorrow, he'll be all right.

"No, he won't be all right. Not tomorrow. Not the day after. What will *he* do tomorrow? Tomorrow, what do *I* do tomorrow? This is our home. We are supposed to be safe."

She turns to the police officers. "Deport me. Send us back home to Afghanistan. It's safer for us there. We came here to be safe, but we're not. We're not safe here."

I can't say anything. I don't know what to say, because I'm afraid she's right.

Skewed Perspective and Burnout

It's a pretty stressful job and there is a high level of burnout among medics. We see enough terrible things that when we hear whining about nothing, and we hear a lot of whining about nothing, we just don't have the patience for it.

A lot of the medics working in Toronto don't actually live in Toronto. They drive in from the 'burbs and many don't even like the city. Before this job, I never understood this. I was born and raised downtown, my friends have always been from downtown and I went to school downtown. I'm a pretty urban guy and I've always been happy about it. It's funny that I call it downtown; it shows how my perspective has changed. I never used to say downtown, because I mostly grew up around Pape and Danforth, which I don't consider downtown. On this job, however, you meet people who say they're from Toronto and when you ask what part they say, "Brampton," so The Danforth starts to feel pretty central.

Anyway, doing this job means that you see a different, darker, seedier side of the city than I am used to, despite growing up here. I was never a big dancing-in-clubs-guy so my experiences with the Docks and the club district are entirely work related and revolve around overdoses and violence. I've treated too many patients and heard too many stories of random people being beaten in clubs because they looked at someone the wrong way or intervened on unwanted advances.

After a while, you start to see everything as dangerous or a potential weapon: bottles, drinking glasses, stairwells. Everyone in a bar has a bottle in his or her hand and I can tell you, from being a witness, that a broken bottle to the throat can cause a lot of damage. This is how people on the job, who are not from Toronto, see the whole city. I've experienced a lifetime of good times here, and I've seen some unpleasant things on the job, but I still know what the city is really all about. Despite doing the job I do and thus knowing what dangers the city has to offer, I rarely feel unsafe.

Before paramedicine, I worked with street youth, homeless adults and people with mental illnesses; a lot of the same population I work with in the ambulance. At that time, I dealt with the same people everyday and they, like all people, had good days and bad days. In the ambulance you only deal with people on their bad days. You don't see the psych patients on good days when they've been taking their meds and they make sense. You don't see the junkies unless they overdose, so they become just that, another overdose. You don't get to talk to the drunk when he's sober. You don't ever find out about the life he had before the alcohol took over. Unfortunately, in the ambulance you tend to see them less as people and more as issues, because you are only interacting with them in one context.

There are some people who call the ambulance so often that you know them by name. Where it really gets weird is when you start to learn their birthdays. This helps when they are unconscious. It also helps to understand them that I speak Pirate.

Actually, to their credit, most of the Frequent Flyers don't call the ambulance themselves; it's the bottomless-well-of-concern, ever supportive public that do. These cell phone warriors call from their cars as they drive out of downtown after seeing Miss Saigon or Jersey Boys or whatever other wastefully overpriced spectacle is going on at the time. These do-gooders call from their car to say there is a man unconscious in the park and he may not be breathing.

I understand that if you are from the suburbs and you're not familiar with downtown and you see a homeless person, you get concerned; but try to remember that they've been surviving on the streets longer than you've been driving an SUV. Homeless people do die on the streets; it's tragic and I'm a huge advocate for the homeless and the right to safe shelter. However, if you really think that they might not be breathing, you should do CPR. Most 'rubby down' calls are saved with the Clap-of-Life. "Sorry, buddy (clap, clap) you can't sleep here. People think you're dead. It makes dinner conversation awkward."

Most calls for an unconscious male downtown are really drunk homeless men. Bringing them to a hospital where they lie for hours in off-load delay, pissing on my stretcher until they sober up enough to verbally abuse me and then either start a fight or quietly stumble away, is not a good use of our healthcare budget. There is a greater social issue of mental illness and addiction that needs to be addressed and it doesn't happen in the emergency room.

We got a call for a man "*repeatedly falling down*" in Allan Gardens which is a park downtown that is very near to many homeless shelters. On a warm night, it becomes a safer, quieter alternative to the shelter system. We circled the park and saw many people '*comfortably down*', but nobody trying to get back up again. The caller had already left the scene and was probably halfway to the 401 where he would feel proud of himself that he had done his good deed for the day. I imagined calling Dispatch to ask for a bus for this mass-casualty situation. "There must be at least 50 men down in the park. My partner is initiating triage. Send me every unit you have!! We need more toe-tags. Repeat: More toe-tags."

Some people call it quits at the one-year mark. They wet their feet and it isn't for them. There are a few legendary stories of newbies walking into the home of an especially bad Code 5, turning around, walking out and getting on a streetcar never to be seen again.

The next wave for jumping ship comes after five years. At the five-year mark, they've tried it and gotten good at it, but they don't want to do it forever. They take the skills they learned here and apply it to another job. At 10 years, if you're young enough, you see the writing on the wall that you'll be here forever and that either sends you into a tail spinning depression that results in quitting, or the complacent acceptance of your fate that I've heard near-drowning victims explain.

Depending on how old you are, the golden handcuffs are pretty well locked after 15 years. If you can survive past the 15-year mark, you are a lifer. The pension and health-care plan start looking too good to leave. At this point you see a lot of people who should leave, but won't, because after you've done this for a while, you feel like you've invested too much of yourself to quit; besides that, you don't feel qualified to do anything else.

Schedule

Every EMS service has a different schedule; so obviously we *must* have chosen the best one.

In January of 2013 we had what was called, "The Great Shuffle" where all familiarity was thrown aside and every medic had to choose a new schedule, colour platoon and station. You'll note that you can't actually choose your partner, which is arguably the most important factor of all for on-the-job happiness. Your partner is the person in the same station with the same schedule so you ride on the same ambulance. Once you own your station and schedule, you are at the mercy of someone else choosing the same schedule and station thus making them your new partner. We say that you don't choose your partner, but your partner chooses you.

I said *the* new schedule, but it is actually *eight* new schedules with six colour platoons and is so incredibly complicated that it would literally[*] be a book unto itself to explain it properly. These eight schedules are all different and include: all day shifts, late starts, most weekends, three similar schedules that are each slightly different, but are pretty similar to our old one, (which was explained in previous editions) and mine, which is called Schedule 1, and I'll go into great detail about it later.

This is just a bit of information for your own background knowledge. I won't be hurt if you skip it. My wife thinks this subject is painfully boring and this chapter should be left out. She said that after ten years, she has no

---

[*] I endeavor to use literally accurately and not in place of figuratively. We were handed a 39 page document on 8 ½ X 11 explaining the schedule. I'll send it to you, if you're that interested.

interest in learning my schedule, so why would anyone else? But, I get asked my schedule so often that I thought I should include it. She says that people only ask me about my schedule because they are too afraid to ask about anything else for fear that I'll launch into a bloody story about rotting old people. She might be right; I do tend to do that.

She is right so often that I rarely challenge her opinion. If I'm right about something once in a blue moon, it is nothing to gloat about, so I usually go with whatever she thinks is best. Unfortunately, I'm out on a limb with this chapter because I am defying her advice. I really wish I could think of a way to make it more interesting…

I can't. Damn.

All shifts on all schedules for all paramedics (except those on light duties) are twelve hours. It makes for a long day, but you get your week over quickly, which is nice.

My schedule is called Schedule 1. It is known as the 50/50 split because we do only days or nights from 7-7, either am or pm. Schedule 1 doesn't have a C-shift, AKA late starts (no 9-9, 11-11 or 2-2). The C-shift, for the other seven schedules, covers six shifts over six weeks (with all of the other shifts being 7-7. With six different colour platoons, it means that there is always someone on their C-shift. The purpose of the C-Shift is to have people working over the traditional shift change at 7:00 pm, thus lessening paramedics getting late calls and doing overtime. Each of the other seven schedules has a C-shift, but we don't.

The quick version of Schedule 1 is that, starting on a Friday, we do four nights, two days off, three days, one day off, three nights, two days off, four days and then finally a glorious seven days off. My brother-in-law once said, "You deserve a week off every four weeks. You work hard, it's a stressful job." This may be true, but I get a week off because we work a lot for the other three weeks. Essentially, we work three 56-hour weeks in order to have it balance as a forty-hour week over four weeks. If you were paying attention, you'll have noticed that the math doesn't work. Yes, schedulers noticed that too, so they created what we call "drop days". Twice over twelve weeks, two shifts will be removed from our schedule. So, one night-shift and one day-shift will magically not be there (but never over a weekend). It feels like you got a day off when it sneaks up on you, but really you made up for it by working too many hours overall.

The other seven schedules have six weeks where every week is different, while ours is four weeks with every week being different. The lowest common denominator between Schedule 1 and the rest of the schedules is 12. So we follow a 12-week cycle made up of four repeating cycles where every week is different. This runs parallel to the six-week cycle of everyone else. That means that there is a very obscure pattern about when we, on Schedule 1, overlap with most of the other schedules. This makes it near impossible to predict who else is ever working and who your relief is.

There are only four colour platoons for Schedule 1, which means that we never overlap with other Schedule 1 people on other colours. On the road, I will never see any of my friends, from before The Great Shuffle, who went to other colours on Schedule 1. It kinda makes me sad.

So I only work nights or days. By getting rid of our C-shift, we replaced it with three day-shifts and three night-shifts. Most people hate schedule 1 because there are three more night-shifts than our old schedule. But, for me, I don't like having three more day-shifts. I prefer working nights to days, because I'm just more of a night person.

Also, since I have three kids, and I still like to spend time with them, I see them more on nights. When I work nights, I get home from work around 7:30 am, right when they're waking up. I make them breakfast and take them to school. I sleep during the day and get up for dinner. We eat together and then I go to work. I get to eat two out of three meals with them. There will be a sleepy time around three or four in the morning, but it's pretty manageable.

When I work days, I'm tired every minute of the entire day. On days, I wake up at 5:30 am (which is actually pretty late) and I hate getting up that early. The winter makes it even worse. It's cold and dark when I wake up. I also get home later in the evening after a day shift because we are more likely to get end-of-shift-overtime from a last minute call. When I work day shifts, I see my kids for an hour at most before they go to bed and I don't eat any meals with them. Those days, I don't like. Those days, I remind myself about the week-off coming up.

I feel like I don't get paid to be a paramedic all day. Instead, I get paid to wake up early. I get paid to get out of bed at 5:30 am in the dark, before the furnace has turned on. I get paid a lot for the first 2 hours of my day. After that, I work for free.

Drawbacks of Being a Paramedic

One of the major drawbacks of being a paramedic is that you can never call 911 for an ambulance –especially for yourself. You have to be pretty sick before you need more than just a drive, and if all you need is a drive, your colleagues may tell you that you should have taken a cab.

If I were to call an ambulance (and I have), first I would make a call directly to Dispatch and, after giving my location, I'd say, "Hypothetically, if I were to call an ambulance right now, who would you send and how long will it take to get here?"

I'd want to know who was coming before I decided if I should just handle it myself. Every medic out there is fine for *your* family, but I have a higher standard. I know these people too well. I know who came in last in their hire, who comes to work hungover and who is just back from driver's training because of an accident. It doesn't mean they won't do a fine job, but it's a little like finding out a friend of yours used to sell acid to your child's grade-school teacher when they were both in high school; it's okay, it's just weird. Besides, I don't want most medics seeing what a slob I am and how I always have a sink full of dishes.

One time I was out with my wife, Lidia, at a Hakka restaurant on Danforth. Hakka is Chinese-ish food from the Chinese community in India. Chinese food cooked with Indian spices, which makes it very delicious and very spicy. We ordered a chili chicken dish that was supposed to be pretty hot. We've both traveled in India and like spicy food, so it wasn't that adventurous an order for us.

The food comes, and since we are sharing it they put it between us. We each start eating from the same plate from our respective sides of the table. I have my first bite and I can feel the chilies crunching in my mouth. I comment that it is pretty spicy, but Lidia doesn't say anything. I continue eating and repeat that this is a tremendously hot meal, but Lidia says that she doesn't really think so. I am dazzled by her capacity for spiciness and soldier on hiding my distress while crunching through this chili dish.

I don't consider myself especially macho, but I didn't stop eating either. My pride is soon overwhelmed by the war going on in my mouth and I need to stop. My face feels flushed and hot and I'm having trouble breathing. Everything is getting darker and my vision is getting spotty. I'm starting to feel faint.

"Lidia," I say, "don't be scared but I think I'm going to pass out. If I do, just lay me on the floor with my feet up and under NO circumstances… let… *anyone*… call… nine-one… one."

I put my head on the table and keep breathing slowly; all the while reminding Lidia not to let them call an ambulance.

After a little bit, I felt better and we figured out that the restaurant had put all the chilies in a big pile on my side of the plate. I hadn't noticed and instead of stirring them in, which would have spread out the heat, I ate them all in just a few bites.

Can you imagine if paramedics had come to treat me for fainting after eating spicy food? I would be the laughing stock of our service (until the next guy did something really stupid, which, fortunately/unfortunately happens frequently). I could never live it down. I'd have to switch jobs. If another medic ever found me unconscious on the floor of a restaurant after eating too spicy a dinner, I'd wake up nasally intubated wearing a diaper with detailed pictures posted on a website devoted to me.

First Aid on a Film Set

When I was a student, I worked for a private ambulance service that was responsible for first-aid on film sets. Anyone who knows anything about film-sets knows that they are incredibly boring. They say there are two things that you are better off not knowing how they get made: movies and hot dogs[*]. But, I grew up on film sets, so I know my way around and actually get a kick out of seeing all the activity (or inactivity).

Unless someone gets hurt, no one really knows or cares about first-aid. You can be pretty well anywhere, but the secret to, not only surviving, but thriving on a set is to know where to park your self.

The best thing about film sets is the food. Napoleon Bonaparte said, "an army marches on its stomach[β]" and so does a film crew. The meals are always lavish and wonderful and there are always snacks to be had, although I should clarify what I mean by snacks. In my regular life, I would happily eat what they call snacks forever. Warm full meals of snacks are at the ready for anyone hungry, after all a well-fed crew is less likely to complain and file a grievance (TEMS should make a note here). Unfortunately, most people on-set are too busy to take advantage of the food; they are, what we in the biz call, 'working'.

The first-aid station is neither busy nor really even working. Well, technically I'm working, but I'm not doing too much. Certainly nothing that interferes with eating. My

---

[*] On 30 Rock, they said "laws and hotdogs", which I thought was funny, because it is a TV show.

[β] Actually, Napolean didn't speak English that well (kind of a sensitive subject), he said, "c'est la soupe qui fait le soldat", which translates closer to "It's the soup that makes the soldier." Still, not bad.

style is to park myself at Craft Services and just eat all day. Craft Services is the crew responsible for food. They will have a mobile truck filled with food called, the Honey Wagon. Working first-aid is a great job. No one ever gets hurt and I gain ten pounds a day.

This day I've been on set for 10 hours standing in one place eating warm delicious sandwiches. Though being so sedentary has made me quite bored and my brain has hardened. I see two women playing a board game off to the side and presume them to both be actors because one was dressed the same as the stuntwoman that I was there "to keep safe" and the other was incredibly gorgeous. I'm shy so I don't approach them and I continue to stand in one place eating. They see me standing there and start calling me over. As it turns out they are playing this game called Taboo and they need four people to do it in two teams of two. The problem with film sets is that even though it appears as if nothing is happening, everyone is really quite busy, so these women were having trouble finding two other people to stay in the game.

They find a partner for me and we start playing. The way Taboo works is that you have to get your partner to say a certain word, but a list of relevant words is taboo and you can't say them. For example, your word or phrase could be 'snow', but you're not allowed to say: white, ice, winter, fluffy, frozen or other related words that are on the list. This forces you to say, "It's a crystalized precipitation that falls, seasonally, from the sky when it's cold✤."

✤ I had time to prepare such a concise sentence. Normally, it would be funnier, more frantic and silly.

The two actors are partners and I'm playing with a rotating and ever-changing temporary partner made up of any crewmember able to spare a minute.

We had been playing for half an hour when, in an attempt to elicit the word 'comedy', the gorgeous woman says to her partner, "Suddenly Susan was…" Her partner says, "Cancelled!!" and bursts out laughing. The next turn was for the other woman to provide the clue and the word was 'autograph' so she says, "Brooke, Brooke, Brooke. Can I have your…" I start detecting a deeper meaning in these two clues and look closer for a connection. With my impressive deductive skills (I regularly ruin the ending of Sherlock, much to my son Lukie's fury), I realize that I actually recognize both of them.

With a few more minutes of pondering, I conclude that I've been playing Taboo all this time with Rosie Perez and Brooke Shields. Maybe it was the exhaustion or all the free food weighing down my senses, but I swear I didn't recognize either of them. Brooke Shields is so much more beautiful in person than on television. This was before her plastic surgery· and post-natal depression. Without all the makeup and everything, she is just a truly naturally beautiful person. There is a reason she is such an icon.

Now that I've clued in, I'm all nervous and stupid and I transform into a complete blathering idiot. It's embarrassing, but I can't help it; I saw Blue Lagoon at a very impressionable age. Before, I was just happy to be talking to someone and now I'm self-conscious, mumbling and can't carry on a conversation. I find myself

· My friend Matt denies that she ever had plastic surgery. Certainly the internet gives the impression that she is against it, but I just call it as I see it. I mean, she's still beautiful, but have you looked at her lately? There has been some kind of intervention.

awkwardly/faux-casually finding a reason to put my hand on her shoulder and then in my mind, I'm doing a happy dance that I've touched Brooke Shields. I wish I hadn't clued in, because now I'm blowing my only chance of semi-normal social interaction. I struggle to remain cool and continue playing the game but my sudden lack of social skills is obvious. They clearly sense the difference and make an excuse to end the game. Dejected, I go back to my sandwiches.

The show was on TV eventually. I saw part of it, but I didn't think it was very good.

Life Imitates Art

One dark and dreary night we got a call for a 16-year-old girl bleeding from the mouth. '*Bleeding from the mouth*' is a very general term that can mean anything from bleeding gums to esophageal varices (blood vessels which burst in your throat and blood pours from your mouth like a broken faucet). I've had both of those calls, and even though one leaves you on the brink of death from exsanguination and the other requires better flossing, they both come in as 'bleeding from the mouth'.

The pager also says she lost '*a lot* of blood', which tells me nothing at all. People on scene always say that the patient has, 'lost a lot of blood', regardless of how much blood has actually left their body.

I try to explain to people that when you give blood at a blood bank, they take a pint of blood and all they give you for treatment is a glass of orange juice and a cookie. I also tell them that if you take a pint of water and pour it on the floor, it will spread over a pretty large area and appear like a lot more water than it actually is. This rarely makes anyone feel better (they are too distracted by the pool of blood to hear any logic), but I say it anyway.

We arrive and the patient's mother calmly directs us to the bathroom. We enter the bathroom and see a sight so shocking that it freezes us in our tracks. The patient is hanging limply over the edge of the bathtub with her back to us. There is blood everywhere. There are bloody handprints on the walls, the sink, the toilet, and all over the tub. The shower curtain has been torn down and lies crumpled on the ground. It looks like an incredibly bloody murder scene. The mother who directed us in doesn't appear to be that concerned, which only makes it scarier.

While my partner and I are standing in stunned silence, in what appears to be a crime scene, the girl suddenly stands up, raises her arms, stumbles towards us and moans. As she opens her mouth blood spills down her already blood-soaked chest. She is as pasty and as pale as a ghost with dark black circles under her eyes. Her arms are extended, blindly reaching for us. She is mumbling something, which I interpret as "brains."

My partner and I are petrified with terror. This would be scary at the best of times, but we had just been watching a zombie movie at the station with lots of blood, gore and brain eating. Shaun of the Dead is still fresh in our minds. I don't feel like I need to make any excuses, but I might have pooed a little.

We discover that she had gone to the hospital earlier that day to have her adenoids removed. When she got home, she had started bleeding from the throat so they went to Emergency. The emerge doctor told her to drink some cold water and it would stop on its own. It didn't. She had no blood pressure and passed out on our stretcher. We went back to the same hospital so that the same doctor could see the results of his expert advice.

Our Jackets

It's the little things that remind me that my job is kind of odd. Little things that seem normal to me that surprise other people. For example: our rain jacket. It was issued to me in 2004 and it's a pretty standard raincoat except that the advertising tag that hangs on the sleeve says, "Protex 2000 series. Waterproof. Breathable. Windproof. Bloodborne Pathogen Safe."

Bloodborne. Pathogen. Safe. I feel so much better doing my job knowing that my jacket is bloodborne pathogen safe. Then I think, "Who would ever want a job where they give you a jacket that brags it is bloodborne pathogen safe?" Really.

On the other side of the tag there is a picture of blood being repelled off the fabric. It's a cute picture.

Being assaulted

So far (touch wood), I've never been hurt by any of the violent drunk people I've had to deal with. Mostly, because when they want to hit you, you see it coming a mile away. First, they get a certain look in their eye; they squint a little as if trying to figure out who you are. Then, once they decide they don't like you, they cock their arm back to hit you and, with a tremendously laboured effort, take a swing. By the time they get to this point, however, it's taken so long that you've stepped out of the way and made a sandwich with all the extra time.

The one time· I did get hit was by a 70-year-old man who had fallen down the stairs and had a head injury. He was a big guy who, despite his age, was in excellent shape and was very strong. He was flat on his back as I was kneeling over him preparing the C-collar for his spinal precautions when he cold cocked me right across the jaw. I didn't even see it coming. A complete sucker punch. His right fist hooked me square in the face, sent me reeling and very nearly knocked me out. I saw stars and everything. Head injury patients can become violent. We call it 'combative'. I'm much more careful now.

· This story is from my first year. I have since had a knife pulled on me, been in a full-on-punch-'em-up-hockey-style-fight, been spat in the face, rolled on the ground wrestling and many other minor scuffles that aren't memorable. I've only pressed charges twice. I'm still very careful.

Clara and the Poo

The call comes in as, "81 year-old female. Alpha sick-person. Patient defecated on floor." We think the last little addition was probably unnecessary, but we always appreciate a warning when there is poo involved.

It's three o'clock in the morning and we pull up to a nice post-war bungalow-style home in the Woodbine and Queen area. The home is clean and proper outside, but obviously hasn't been renovated since it was built. It is clearly the home of an old person. The front door is unlocked, so we call out and enter. The inside is just as neat and proper. An elderly woman's voice comes from the other side of the house.

"Oh thank goodness you're here. I'm so embarrassed."

My partner is attending, so he does the talking. "What's the problem tonight, ma'am?"

"I had an accident on the floor. Clean it up, please."

"We'll deal with your accident in a minute. How are you feeling?"

"Oh, I'm fine. Just embarrassed. Clean it up and you can be on your way."

"Are you feeling sick? Do you have any medical problems?"

"No, no. I'm fine. I just didn't make it to my toilet in time. I'm so embarrassed. Clean it up so I can go to bed."

We make our way to the kitchen and there in the middle of the kitchen floor is a perfectly formed, and impressively large, pile of poo.

"You called for an ambulance because there is poo on the floor? There is nothing else wrong with you? "

"I didn't call the ambulance. I called Lifeline. I push this button and a lady comes on the speaker and helps me."

"You didn't call 911?"

"No. I just spoke to the lady on the speaker."

"You called Lifeline."

"Yes."

"I want to talk to Lifeline."

"Sure, It's easy. I'll just push the button."

On her wrist is a bracelet with a button on it. When she pushes it, a speakerphone automatically starts dialing a phone number. After 2 rings, an automated voice answers.

"Thank you for calling Lifeline..."

"Oh, there she is now. Hello..."

"...Please hold and one of our operators will be with you shortly."

"Okay," then to us, "she's just getting someone."

The automated message continues, "Sorry for the delay..."

"I understand," says our patient.

"... an operator will be with you shortly."

"Okay," she replies. Then she looks from the phone to us, "she's very nice, but they get busy."

After a few rings the human Lifeline operator picks up the phone.

"Hello, this is Lifeline. Have the paramedics come yet, Clara?"

My partner steps in to speak with the operator. "Yes. I'm with the ambulance. Are you the one who called the paramedics for poo on the floor?"

"We tried to contact the family first, but they were unavailable."

"So are you the one who called 911 and decided it was a medical emergency that she had poo on her floor?"

"We made every effort to contact the family first, but they were unavailable."

"I believe that they were unavailable. It's three o'clock in the morning and who wants to come and clean poo off the floor at the best of times? So was it you that decided to call the ambulance and utilize 911 emergency services to clean poo off the floor?"

"Our system is to contact the family first and if they are unavailable to send an ambulance."

"I understand. That makes sense if you have a medical emergency, but did you believe there was any medical emergency or did you only call us to clean poo off her floor."

"She pushed her Lifeline assistance button and we made every effort to contact her family first..."

"Did you think that she was having a medical emergency or a housekeeping emergency? Do you personally believe that poo on the floor requires an ambulance? Do you think that everyone with something to clean up should call 911?"

There is silence on the line while the woman from Lifeline prepares her next thought. "We were concerned that she might slip on the poo and hurt herself. If she fell and hit her head or broke her hip *after* you leave it could become a very serious medical emergency."

My partner has nothing to say back. I watch as the gears of liability turn in his head. She has verbally warned us of a hazard on a taped phone line and she is absolutely right that if Clara slips and falls after we were at her home and didn't take her to the hospital, we'll lose our jobs.

After a triumphant pause, she says, "Thank you for calling Lifeline." Click. The phone goes dead. My partner is livid. He takes a few deep breaths. I can almost read his lips as he counts to ten before he speaks again. No doubt something he learned in anger management classes.

He turns to Clara and steels himself up for what he is going to say next. In his most gravelliest three-am-voice he says, "Okay. Let's clean up that poo."

"Good. I already have a plan," she says sweetly, almost enthusiastically. I should have been suspicious that she had a plan already in place. "Use the dustpan and broom. Scoop it up and drop it in my toilet." She has a mobile toilet on wheels that she keeps in the kitchen.

"Where," my partner asks, his energy waning, "is your dust pan?"

"The dust pan is in the closet."

I wait with Clara and listen to him shuffling around in the kitchen. We hear him in the closet moving around the cleaning implements. We hear him clearing his throat and grunting as he scoops the poo.

"Okay. I'm putting it into your toilet." We hear the sound of poo landing in her mobile commode.

"Thanks. Now make sure it's all up. Use a cloth to wipe it up."

"Where do I find a cloth?" he calls from the other room.

"Use the wet yellow cloth that is under the sink."

"I found a white one"

"Keep looking. Use the yellow one. It's already wet." We hear the sink door open again. Clara and I wait while he continues to rummage around under her sink.

"Okay, I found a yellow cloth, but it's not wet."

"Yes, it is."

"Ma'am, I'm holding it and I can assure you that it isn't wet."

"Are you sure?"

"Positive. Neither cloth is wet."

"I was so sure I already wet it."

"You might have. Wet things tend to dry with time. I can wet it again." He is sounding more and more tired by the minute.

"Well, I guess you'll have to re-wet the yellow one. Go ahead, wet the yellow one."

"Ok." He wipes the bit of residual poo off the floor with the yellow cloth that he has freshly moistened in the sink.

"Now throw away the yellow cloth. Throw it away."

"OK." He tries to exit the kitchen.

"Dry it with the white cloth."

"Excuse me?"

"Use the white cloth to dry the wet spot where you cleaned with the yellow cloth. You said the white cloth is dry, right?"

"The floor really isn't wet."

"I don't want to slip. You dry it with the white cloth."

"OK."

"Now put the white cloth in the laundry hamper by the stairs. I'll wash that and reuse it. It was only drying water."

By now I'm amazed that my partner hasn't blown an aneurism. He tends to not be patient at the best of times and this woman is really pushing it. Amazingly, he stays calm the whole time and we leave after making sure that there isn't anything else that we can do for her.

We thought the story would end there, but one week later we get a call to the same address, for the same woman, again in the middle of the night. The call information says, "82 year-old female. Assistance with walker." We recall the incident of cleaning up the poo and grumble about taking a blood pressure on a walker.

We find her standing in her living room. She turns to us with a mixture of relief and desperation and says, "Thank goodness you're here. My sweater got caught in my walker. I can't move and I really have to POO!"

We are well aware that she is fully capable, and perhaps even ready and willing to poo right there on the floor, so we don't waste time. We free the sweater from the wheels of her walker and toss both aside. We each take one of her shoulders and carry her to the kitchen where we know she keeps her toilet. This is all done with great speed and efficiency because we know that she is prone to pooing on the floor and we also know that she isn't shy about asking us to clean it up. We get her seated, pull down her panties (at her request), and move ourselves around the corner to the living room so that she can do her business in the privacy of her open concept kitchen.

From the kitchen we hear her call, "It was my birthday yesterday. There's cake on the table. Help yourself."

My partner has lost his appetite, but I'm a sucker for a good chocolate cake.

First Time Drinkers

We got a call to the club district for a 25-year-old male HBD (Has Been Drinking). We arrive to find him sitting slouched on the ground in an alley off of Richmond. One of the last places I would ever sit on the ground is in an alley off the club district. The pukeable proximity to all the major clubs is just too close. I would have trouble forgetting the volume of people who have stumbled into this alley solely for the purpose of puking, peeing, bleeding or having sex with strangers. Even if I were able to ignore my natural aversion to the growing Petri dish of human waste that is spread across the alley's floor, I would still be too distracted by the seemingly unending number of people who don't share my standards of distaste and frequent the alley for their own purposes to be able to relieve myself comfortably.

This alley has the usual layer of a weekend's accumulation of bodily fluids with the bonus factor of being flanked by a restaurant, so there is a deeper and more widespread layer of rotting food. It appears that the giant green-bin dumpster either leaks, or has been rendered obsolete by the more convenient option of simply throwing food directly to ground where it can compost without delay.

Our patient is still relatively upright as he sits on the ground; he's swaying but not face-planting, yet. He has maintained the décor of the alley by vomiting all over himself and the ground around him. My first thought is, "I don't want that in my ambulance."

His friends are panicking and very concerned that he is dying. They are trying to be helpful in the way that only extremely drunken friends are known to be. They are all talking at once, pointing in every direction, telling me obscure childhood medical facts and trying to shake my hand to thank me for helping. They are going through the typical emotional stages that one goes through when one is piss-drunk and worried about a friend: each of the eight men in their early 20s are rotating through: concern, fear, apology, encouragement and declaring their love for the patient. This manifests itself as crying, yelling, hugging and high-5s. I am the victim of these as much as the patient.

The story is that this is a group of friends who, for religious reasons, don't normally drink alcohol. They were going out for someone's birthday and thought that in the spirit of celebration, they would forsake their God and try alcohol for the first time. I guess one of them developed a taste for it and wanted to show off his capacity for shooters. He wasn't aware of things like pacing, so considering the sin was already done and in order to maximize his night of elected debauchery, he drank hard and fast.

I explain to the friends that these are the normal, expected, and perceived as pleasant, effects of excessive alcohol. I further explain that he is doing fairly well considering he can still protect his airway and can sit without falling over. They ask what they can do for him and what stages will come next. I tell them to take him home, because the next stage is that he hits on someone's girlfriend, gets into a fight and then really gets hurt.

Family Barbecue

This is actually pretty awful.

We get called to an outdoor family reunion in North York to find a man flat on his back beside an overturned ladder. There is chaos as more than a dozen family members are running around scared and panicked. There is an acrid burning smell in the air. I deduce that in the confusion, the barbeque has been neglected and dinner is burning.

The story is that the Dad had seen a raccoon in a tree and decided to take that moment to get rid of it. Using a metal ladder, he climbed up to try and hit the raccoon with a metal pole. We don't know what personal issue he had with one of God's little creatures, but for some reason he was very intent and focused on relocating the raccoon at that moment.

Unfortunately, he wasn't focused on the power lines that ran through the tree. He missed the raccoon and hit the power lines sending mucho volts in through his hands and out through his thighs and shins which were in contact with the very well grounded ladder.

The burning smell gets stronger and I start thinking that it just doesn't smell right. At first I thought it was the burgers being left to burn and then I clue in that the burning flesh smell isn't the barbie, it's my patient.

The moral of the story is: Don't mess with raccoons.

Balcony Lady

Sometimes when we are en route to a call, we'll strategize a little. For example, to a VSA we might decide who is on the airway and who is on the defibrillator, or we might review protocols for expected death or the dosage of epinephrine for a child with croup. We might say to each other, "you go straight in with the bags while I turn around the vehicle so that we can leave faster." Or in a public place, "you deal with the patient and I'll pick us up some sandwiches." Most calls, however, require no pre-planning and are simply routine. Waking up a drunk for example, is one of those calls; although, even those calls often have a twist…

We got a call for a 28-year-old woman who had been drinking and was unable to walk in her living room. Being drunk and then unable to walk is really the job security for a downtown medic. This requires no pre-planned strategy on our part and is usually an easy call. The idea is to provoke them into standing up, get them to stumble towards us and then have them collapse on the stretcher, preferably already in the ambulance. They don't teach it in school, but it works. If you were to stray from having the drunk walk up or down the stairs on his own steam, you'd be quickly corrected by your partner.

The house is a triplex and she is on the second floor. We found her in the living room, drunk and unable to get up off the floor. She's a big girl, maybe 375 lbs. Although she *was* very drunk, we discovered that the real reason she couldn't get up was less because of the alcohol and more because she had broken both her legs.

This is the story: She lives on the second floor with her boyfriend and their three children. She was taking care of the kids that evening while he was out doing something to make the world a better place, or maybe to buy more beer.

Because she was in this position of responsibility, she got really drunk with the people on the third floor. Wondering how the children were, she decided that she should check on them and make sure that they were okay. In a sudden panic, while still on the third floor, she realized that she didn't have her keys. Using drunken logic·, she decided that she should climb over the balcony and jump down to the second floor fire escape.

As her friends continued to sip on bottled-wisdom, nobody intervened on this act of heroism and she jumped. Did I mention that she's a big girl? She blew out both sets of tib-fibs. Using booze as a painkiller, she dragged herself into the living room and called us.

· There is a lot of talk and public information about drinking-and-driving, drinking-and-dialing, inebre-mailing and even faced-facebooking, but not so much about drinking-and-thinking, which is arguably the root of all alcohol related accidents and embarrassments.

We find her on the floor, hobbled like the guy in *Misery*. "How did you get in?" she asks.

"What do mean?" we reply. "The door was open?"

That's the Ticket

We get a call to a sleazy apartment building on Sherbourne for a Code 5. He is described as *VERY* dead by the superintendent who found him. The super was checking the apartment because the tenant below had complained that there was water flowing through the ceiling. The super checked the apartment upstairs and found a dead man in the kitchen. The sink was left running and water was overflowing throughout the apartment. I've never understood why kitchen sinks don't have overflow protectors the way bathroom sinks do. It seems like a good idea.

You really find out how uneven a floor is when you let it fill with water; parts of the apartment are more than ankle deep, while others are bone-dry. A cat was stranded in one dry corner. It was afraid to walk through the water so my partner, who generally likes animals more than he likes people, (exception: unattainably attractive women) rescued the cat from the corner and set it up in a larger, drier area with a fresh litter box and some food.

The occupant is indeed very, very dead - maybe a day or two. He is crumpled in front of his sink with a broken drinking glass on the floor. The apartment is tiny and very sparsely furnished. No pictures of any people. Not well kept. He didn't own many objects. There are medicine containers on the counter: heart, breathing, pain – lots of serious meds. We find a binder from Princess Margaret which was tracking his palliative care for cancer. This was a very sick dude. It all seems very natural but police are required, because I'm not a crime scene guy and I can't make that call in the same way that firefighters aren't medical guys; except that, unlike them, I don't try to be a crime scene guy.

A cop comes and asks us our opinion on the medical side of him being dead. We tell him it all appears consistent. The three of us are standing in the living room when I notice that my partner's eyes dart to the coffee table and focus on something. The cop and I follow his gaze to find a lottery ticket. No one moves as our eyes flick from one to another. If this were a spaghetti western, there would be ever increasing close-ups of our eyes. With sweat forming on our temples, one of us would be chewing a toothpick while another one of us would probably have an iron stove-door hidden under his shirt. It's like the end of *Reservoir Dogs* as we stare each other down, waiting for someone to make the first move.

We're all thinking the same thing, "What if this ticket is a winner?" What if he found out he won, walked to the kitchen for a celebratory glass of water and then had a heart attack from the excitement? Everyone is frozen in place as we share this *Waking Ned Devine* moment. We all want to look at the ticket, but none of us wants to seem obvious about it. Slowly, we all move simultaneously towards the ticket in a triangle of curiosity and mutual distrust. I gently pick it up and look at the date. The draw was the day before. We are all silent, each wondering what the others are thinking. Actually, we all know *exactly* what each other is thinking, we just don't want to admit it out loud. I set the ticket down on table while keeping my eyes on the other two.

"Anyone see a paper around?"

"No."

"Mmmm."

My partner picks it up next, then the cop. We each want to see the numbers for ourselves as if it'll say, "*Winner!*" on it. We remain perfectly still as we stand around the ticket.

"Did you see any signs of family? Any contacts?" the cop asks.

"No."

"Mmmm."

"What happens if this ticket is a winner?" I query.

The cop answers. "If there is no family to claim it, it'll probably be discarded."

"Mmmm."

"So..."

"So..."

"So..."

The tension is palpable as we wait for someone to make a move. The cop breaks the silence. "You got everything you need?" There is another more awkward silence. My partner and I accept that we have no reason to stay there any longer. The cop knows this too.

I pick up the ticket again. "I'm just going to write these numbers down... Just curious. And..." I add casually, as if it were an after thought, "What's your name and PC number? For, you know... the paper work." He tells me his badge number and I read his name off his ID.

My partner and I slowly work our way to the door. "Well, I'll be watching the numbers and if your name comes up, you'll be getting a phone call... Heh, heh." I say half joking, but with obvious serious intent.

There are a few jokes about quitting work and bank accounts in the Cayman Islands. We all laugh awkwardly as my partner and I walk out the door.

Hellooooo

I'm in the ambulance on a night shift. It is around 2:00 am, when I hear a strange male voice come over the air on the trunk radio.

"Helloooo. Hellooooooo"

"Last unit calling. Go ahead," the dispatcher replies, obviously annoyed that the caller is not using proper ambulance radio protocols. I'm not going to judge because I've been known to flex the rules when it comes to on-air communication and etiquette. While I was on truck number 4252, I was spoken to by a supervisor once when, to the chorus of *(I Feel Like a) Natural Woman*, I announced my arrival at St Micheal's Hospital by singing:

"Four-two-five-two…
Four-two-five-two…
Four-two-five-two, forty-two-fifty-two is ten-sev-en
At Saint Mi-ii-ii-ikes."

If it has been quiet and there hasn't been anything too major, then things can get pretty giddy on a night shift·. Some medics hate anything that isn't proper formal on-air communication, which I understand, but on occasion, I like to have a little fun. It's about more than just making the night go faster; it makes the *years* go faster.

There is a proper way that we're supposed to do things and I respect that, mostly. I too, have been frustrated by on-air chatter when I really needed some air-time.

I was once in a situation where I needed police assistance in a rush. We arrived at a psychiatric patient's

---

· Recently, a Dispatcher was heard using his Elmer Fudd voice on-air. It was awesome.

house and we were told by a room-mate that he had left. This meant we could take a little break before we had to check in with dispatch to tell them, "No patient found". We drove around the corner to put our feet up and have a snack when a man flagged us down. We approached the man without updating dispatch on our status and our new location. This man turned out to be our missing patient. He became increasingly agitated to the point of violence and we decided that we needed the police. While the two of us wrestled with the patient, I tried to have this conversation with dispatch on the portable radio.

"4067. I need 10-200's in a rush. I'm at Abbott and Johnson."

"4067. You are 'where' and Johnston?"

"Abbott."

"Arbour?"

"Abbott."

"Norbet?"

I realized that I needed to spell it. When I passed my Restricted Radio Operator's License I knew the entire fancy military alphabet, but since then, I only use Alpha to Echo regularly and I've forgotten most of the rest. This was a pretty urgent situation and I didn't have time to concentrate and burrow through the deep recesses of my memory, so I spelled it as best as I could.

"I am at Johnson and Abbott. Spelled: Apple, Banana, Banana, Ornella, Tomato, Tomato."

"I copy Johnson and Abbott, 4067, the 200's are on the way."

I did pretty well using fruits, a vegetable (or another fruit depending on who you ask) and the name of another paramedic who was on duty that night. I used to know all the phonetic alphabet, but over time it has started slipping. I think I got perfect when I took my Restricted Radio

Operator's License, though I probably cheated. No doubt I had the alphabet written on my forearm or something ridiculous like that. At least Hotel and whatever 'J' stands for.

But I digress. Back to this story…

"Hellllooooooooo" comes the voice again.

We are supposed to identify ourselves every time we speak on the air, so this time the dispatcher ignores him. She doesn't want to get drawn into this game at this hour of the night.

"Hellllloooooooooooooo. Can you hear me? Hellllooooooooooo."

"Last unit, go ahead." Reluctantly she plays into answering this bizarre way of calling the dispatcher.

"Hellooo?"

"**Go ahead**." The dispatcher is obviously annoyed.

"Hello. I think somebody left this here by accident. It's a walkie-talkie."

There are several ways that we communicate with dispatch. The main two are the communication radios. One is called the *trunk radio* and is located in the ambulance and the other is called the *portable radio*. As the name implies, we carry the portable around with us whenever we are out of the vehicle. This would be on a call, in a hospital, pretending that we're mobile or when we go shopping. We also have pagers and the ALS Medics are trusted with cell phones, but those are irrelevant to this story.

"Hellooo. I'm in a Pizza Nova at Eglinton and Bermundsey. Helloooooo. Can you hear me? Two paramedics left this walkie-talkie here. There was a big man and a little girl. Hellooo. I need to close the store. Hellooo."

Now we all understand what's going on. Not just all the paramedics in the city that share the south-east channel, but all the tow-truck drivers and TV news people that listen in on scanners.

Dispatch has call display for the radios so they know which truck's portable has been talking this whole time, but the rest of us don't and we're all really curious to find out which crew left a multi-thousand dollar piece of equipment in a Pizza Nova.

There is radio silence for a long minute and then another ambulance comes on using their trunk radio.

"4999 call," the paramedic asks, sheepishly.

"4999, go ahead." You can hear the dispatcher smile over the air.

"Can we go to Eglinton and Bermundsey for... a personal service?"

"Sure 4999. That's probably a good idea."

The Obesity, Nudity, Poo Triad

Obese. Nude. Covered in poo. Most people would be amazed at how often these three seemingly independent items go together when servicing 911 calls.

Maybe it's because we don't have very good blinds at home, but I don't walk around my house naked. I just don't. It's not that I'm afraid to, I just always have some clothes nearby and I like wearing them. Apparently, a lot of people don't feel that way. We do calls for naked people all the time. Daily. I offer them clothes and they say, "no thanks." I remind them that they will need clothes to *leave* the hospital. They still decline. I throw their clothes and shoes in a bag anyway.

A lot of people die naked, which is something else that I've never understood. Why can't people at least wear underwear? Is it so hard? I've never thought to keep a record of it, but it seems that most people get naked before they die. I don't know why. If I ever have the sudden desire to lock all the doors, get naked, walk to the third floor, wedge myself between the toilet and the wall in a narrow two-piece bathroom and cover myself in poo, I'll know that I am about to die.

When medics gripe about obesity, it isn't a question of body image or attractiveness. It is simply a matter of the logistics of lifting, since obese people tend to be heavier than other people. In our job, people are usually either obese or withered and sticklike. There is precious little in between. That is just the nature of the people who tend to be in need of medical services. Occasionally, we'll get a patient who is relatively healthy and sane, but believe me, it's not the norm.

One day, we got a call for a woman unconscious in bed. We were warned before getting there that she was in excess of 350 pounds.

We arrived to find that she wasn't unconscious so much as just unable to get out of bed due to her volume/energy ratio. She is naked and sized as advertised. Because she was confined to bed for a few days, she had been doing little more than pooing in bed and then rolling in it. As we struggled to get her out of bed there was much grabbing and prodding. Despite my best efforts to wrap her and myself in sheets, there was always another fold containing a hidden cache of poo and I got it on myself. It was all very upsetting, for us, so after the call was completed, we went back to the station to shower and do a complete uniform change.

Bathing and changing can only go so far in a case of PTSD so when the station phone rang for another call, I answered it like this. "As long as she isn't obese, naked and covered in poo, I'm ready for another."

"How about: obese, naked and eating poo?" the dispatcher replies dryly.

"I can't tell if you're joking."

"I'm not."

If there was a steering wheel, I'd be pounding it and yelling, "Why? Why? Why? Why do I get all the pooey calls?" But the truth is that I know there are more than enough poo calls to go around and, in spite of my day, I don't have a monopoly on them.

The dispatcher comes back to break my stunned shock. "Actually, I'm not sure if this is better or worse, but she isn't eating her own poo. She's eating her cat's poo."

The call turned out to be pretty benign. She was finished eating her cat's poo when we got there and got dressed on her own with little prompting. In fact, she walked to the stretcher, which automatically makes her a pretty favorable patient. Bless her.

Hospital Calls

The funny thing about doing calls in hospitals is that there are all these doctors around, but most of them aren't very useful in an emergency. They went to school for a long time and they are way smart about more medical stuff than I'll ever know, but when someone faints in front of them, they panic and fall apart. I don't give them a hard time though; it isn't their skill set. I just hope they take the moment to recognize that we have some skills too. Many doctors aren't very respectful of our profession.

Most doctors think paramedics are nothing more than truck drivers with first-aid. This is probably because up until the 1960s, paramedics really were only truck drivers with first-aid. Actually, they didn't even drive a truck; they drove either a hearse or a converted (read as re-painted) hearse. Paramedics, or 'ambulance drivers', because they didn't do much else than drive, were employed by funeral homes (hence the hearse) which created an interesting conflict of interest, because the privately run ambulance service/funeral home would be the ones to dispatch the ambulance for a sick or injured person.

If the patient lived, the ambulance driver would take them to the hospital. But if the patient died they would bring them to the funeral home. Bringing dead people to the funeral home created more business for them. This meant it was more profitable to have patients die than to have them live, which of course lessened the incentive for funeral homes to hire people who were skilled in first-aid or even terribly ethical. The saying was, "strong back, weak mind makes for a good ambulance driver."

It has been a hard stereotype to shake, especially for anyone old enough to remember it first hand.

I'm not saying that we're all members of Mensa (or as one *male* patient once bragged, "I'm really smart. I'm a member of menses"), but we have come a long way since the 'scoop and run' style of paramedicine.

All of this is to say that it's satisfying as a lowly paramedic to calmly walk into a situation, like a syncope (fainting) that causes such a panic among physicians. Most of the time the patient is a family member of someone in the hospital and has fainted due to stress, not sleeping and not eating because a loved one is ill. Zebra hunting doctors will think the patient had a massive aneurism while paramedics will ask if they missed breakfast.

The Hospital for Sick Children is even more extreme. Sick Kids is an incredible hospital for children, but when an emergency happens to an adult they get all confused. They have tiny little BP cuffs and tiny little stethoscopes. They are used to children's vital signs so they get all panicky over a pulse of 60 and a BP of 140 over 90.

The Ship's Bell

One time we got a call to Princess Margaret Hospital, or Princess Maggie as I call it.

The call information says, "58-year-old man having an anaphylactic reaction. History of colon cancer. Patient is in chemotherapy recovery room."

Princess Margaret Hospital is *the* cancer hospital to go to. Cancer is all they do, and they are darn good at it. It is state-of-the art, right downtown and the best place to be if you have cancer. But cancer usually attacks pretty slowly, and anaphylaxis happens about as quickly as you can get.

The recovery room is for patients to rest in after having had chemotherapy. A chemo treatment beats the hell out of you and afterwards you need to rest and recover.

This floor is full of people either awaiting chemo, in the process of having it done or resting afterwards. Depending on the cancer and the stage you are in, one usually endures around a bunch of treatments with horrible side effects, which are then followed by the stressful/hopeful phase of waiting to find out if it was effective or not. Sometimes you're cured, sometimes more chemo treatments are required and sometimes you've done all you can do and the next phase is palliative.

We go past recovery-bed after recovery-bed of patients who have just had a chemo treatment. He is at the end of the hall and there are a gaggle of medical professionals gathered around him, all very excited. They are out of their element and are desperately trying to remember things from their far off days in school. They have already given epinephrine and he looks fine now.

On the way out, I see a big bell by the front door. It looks like a ship's bell and I'm tempted to ring it, but I resist. He says to me, "I need to ring the bell. I'm very superstitious. I need to ring the bell. It's my turn. I have to." I wanted to ring the bell myself, so I understand the desire.

We roll the stretcher over to the bell and he rings it good and loud. As soon as he does, the whole floor – staff and patients – all break out into loud enthusiastic applause. If you've ever been with someone going through chemo at Princess Margaret, then you know what was happening. Fortunately, at the time, I never had, so it had to be explained to me.

On your last chemo treatment at Princess Margaret, you get to ring the bell. It signifies that you've finished the painful treatments and now you get to go home, where you will hope and pray that it worked and was all worth it. The support and hope from everyone on that floor was beautiful. They were sharing a common experience and fighting a common enemy. I heard it in the bell and felt it in the applause. I was honoured to have been able to share such a special moment·.

· Between writing this book and printing it, my Dad was diagnosed with inoperable Ampullary Cancer. He only had 2 chemo treatments at Princess Margaret, he didn't get a chance to ring the bell.

Frequent Flyers

Lightning Jim, RIP.
I never really minded taking you to the hospital. You were always pretty good with me, but then again, I knew to offer you an egg-salad sandwich when you'd start getting violent.

The call comes in as "*Delta. Cyclist struck. Patient is lying in the bicycle lane on Gerrard at Horticultural Drive.*" I'm a commuter cyclist so I have a soft spot for the bikers and I would like to see them live because it ups our numbers. We blaze lights and sirens through downtown on a mission to save, who I believe is, another fellow cyclist.

Horticultural Drive is a street that runs through Allan Gardens. Allan Gardens is actually a beautiful part of Toronto that very few people frequent. Those very few however, are there all the time, because they sleep there. The homeless population living in the park is very high and the park is flanked on every side by homeless shelters, which explains the popularity. It's just so darn convenient.

Despite the clientele, it really is a beautiful park with an incredible indoor green house garden that is huge and well worth visiting. There is a whole room devoted to cacti, there are pools with giant goldfish and orchids and everything. It's great, but you'd never know it from the outside.

The homeless people who live in the park are generally the harmless too-drunk-to-hurt-anyone type, so it is actually relatively safe. As the sun goes down, the needles sparkle on the grass in a most becoming way. If you squint just right, it can look like waves on the ocean. Okay, I admit that I'm over romanticizing it, but it's still worth visiting.

We get an update. "*Patient's name is Wayne, lives at Seaton House.*" Seaton House is just down the street from Allan Gardens and is one of the roughest and dodgiest of the homeless men's shelters. Every shelter has its own rules to dictate who can stay there and in what condition. Seaton House seems to have some pretty loose rules. When you are drunk, insane, violent and kicked out of every other shelter in the city, you can usually still stay at Seaton House. Actually, that isn't true; you *can* get kicked out of Seaton House for being too drunk, violent or insane, so they set up another branch of Seaton House to accommodate these men. Conveniently, it is located next door.

Seaton House has a slogan on the front wall that I find quite moving, "Only 3 kinds of men: Someone's Father, Someone's Son and Someone's Brother." Bless them for existing, but curse me for having to go there sober·.

There is a frequent flyer at Seaton House named Wayne Roller. Everybody knows Wayne. There are plenty of nice guys at Seaton House but Wayne is not one of them when he's drunk. He is verbally abusive, violent and always tries to pick a fight with the paramedics. When he's sober, he's fine, but those occasions are few and far between. I have dealt with him when he is drunk far too many times to have any compassion left. Sure enough, as we get closer, I see a man face down in the bicycle lane. There is no bicycle in sight and I'm sure there never was one. The information just got mixed up between the caller and the 911 call-taker.

I see his curly light brown mop of hair and my blood pressure starts to rise. I clench the dashboard a little too

· We have a movement at 40 Station to change the EMS slogan from "People helping people" to "People who *should* be drinking helping people who *have* been drinking."

tightly and start to grind my teeth. It's my turn to attend, but I haven't the patience for him today. It must be obvious because as we approach the scene my partner, bless him, says, "I'll take this one."

In any ambulance-partner relationship, there is often 'the nice one' and 'the mean one'. It isn't planned or anything, it just works out that way. It isn't that the 'mean one' is actually mean or anything like that; it's just that someone has to move the call along when the patient doesn't voluntarily want to get up off the ground. Most of the time you don't need a 'mean one' and being friendly is the way to get things done, but sometimes you have to non-violently motivate/kick a little ass.

So far, with most partners I've ever had (except for new people who are unbearably nice) I have usually been the 'nice one': the one who apologizes for his partner and keeps the complaints away. This, I would like to believe is a syndrome of being relatively new, but my current partner has been on longer than me and is far more patient than I am. In fact, he is so freaking nice• that he makes me look like the mean one·.

It's weird, kind of liberating, but weird all the same. I've never been the 'mean one' before. Generally, I really

---

• I intend this in the kindest possible way. He's a great guy and a fantastic partner. I pity him on a regular basis that he has to put up with me, my personal activites, and all my extra-curricular hobbies. He manages to tolerate me well enough, so maybe he doesn't mind me as much as I would if I were him. I'd drive me crazy.

· Recent events have caused me to conclude that I am not as nice as I previously thought. What's that smell? Is that me getting crispy. I can feel the warm sizzle of becoming burnt out creeping up on me. Can I blame 40? Anyone else would. Damn, I thought I was doing so well.

am about as nice as you can be, but my partner is just a little bit nicer and that turns me into the mean one. Dammit.

We pull the ambulance up next to him and I can't help thinking that we've missed an opportunity to 'accidentally' run him over. In my mind, I consider the repercussions of crushing him beneath the wheels of the ambulance. An incident report? A few visits to court? The other medics would bake me a cake. I ponder my ability to wrangle up some crocodile tears and feign being upset at the death of this man. Despite years of acting, I don't think I'd be able to hide my glee. It's just as well that I'm not driving.

We pull up and the concerned citizens who called 911 are still there. Usually, people who call 911 for drunks just leave. They're concerned, but not enough to actually make contact. I always get a warm satisfaction when they stick around and see how much danger our patient was really in. They called 911 with earnest concern, and I respect anyone who tries to help other people and make the world a better place, so I feel a little bad that their first impression isn't always one of a loving nurturing EMS service[·].

I love, however, the mental process that the caller goes through of having us first appear as uncaring unsympathetic assholes and then the slow realization that

---

[·] I'm fully aware that it is redundant to say EMS service. EMS, of course, stands for Emergency Medical Service so really that sentence should read "... a loving nurturing EM service". But that looks awkward. It's just like asking for your 'SIN number', which is really saying Social Insurance Number number. The truth is I just discovered the 'foot note' feature and was looking for an excuse to use it. This is so much fun. Everyone should write a book.

this patient has been drinking daily and passing out on the street longer than the caller has been wearing a tie and commuting in from the suburbs.

We approach slowly and address him with the 40 Station professionalism that is born from waking up 4 or 5 drunks a day. Forty Station is right downtown and we service the Yonge St core and the club district. We see the socio-economic span of alcoholism and wake them all up the same way. The reactions we get are pretty similar too.

"Wayne, get up!"

"Fuck you, bitch! Suck my cock"

"Wayne! C'mon, these people are worried about you. Get up."

"Fuck you! I'll fuckin' fuck you up, you goof!"

"Wayne. Do you want to go to the hospital or back to Seaton House?"

"Seaton House..."

"Fine. We'll take you there, but you have to be able to walk or they won't take you. Get up."

I reach my hand out to him and pull him to his feet but he staggers and starts to fall down again.

"You're a fuckin' punk-bitch faggot."

"I know Wayne, you've told me before. Let's go."

I wave to the people who called 911. Hopefully they get the idea that, despite their concerns, this patient will out-live us all. If not, I hope they have the 911 service removed from their phone. He's too drunk to go to Seaton House, which is really saying something. We are forced to bring him in to the hospital.

"You're a bitch-fuckin'-asshole-goof."

"I know, Wayne. Let's go."

"I got ADD!!"

The only good thing about Wayne is that we usually don't have to stay with him very long at the hospital. He gets riled up so easily that he usually gets into a fight with someone and gets kicked out by security. Or, once he's sober enough, he just walks out. He rarely stays long enough to get into a hospital bed and be seen by a doctor so I know that this is a complete waste of time, resources and tax dollars.

I'm driving and I can hear the long string of verbal abuses continuing to be laid upon my partner all the way to the hospital. I try desperately to block out everything he's saying, but I can't. I'd turn the radio louder, but I need to be able to hear in case Wayne attacks my partner and they start fighting. Finally, we arrive at the hospital. I come around to the side door to help him out. My partner gives him one last piece of advice.

"Okay Wayne, we're at the hospital. Be nice."

"You're a cunt, bitch. Suck my dick, fucker... I got ADD."

I snap and finally say, "Wayne, ADD is the least of your problems. You're a fuckin' idiot."

He looks at me shocked. His face is frozen in surprise like I just whacked him with a large fish. He stares at me for about 10 seconds, and then starts to cry. It's a real pathetic whimper, "Why'd you have to say that?" He has tears streaming down his face. "What did I ever do to you?"

I deal with some people so regularly that I have their name, birthday, health card number and medical history written in my notebook·. This way if they are completely unconscious I already have all their information. As an added bonus, I don't need to talk to the regulars. I can just throw their urine soaked carcass on my stretcher and drive to the hospital.

Another regular is a gentleman we'll call Steve 'Pain-in-the-ass-ie'. He is another guy that I see way too much. Once we picked him up four times in a 5-day shift and he had been picked up by at least two other crews that we spoke to that week.

We brought him to St Mike's and as we wheeled him in we heard his name being called. It turned out that

---

· I no longer do this because a memo went around stating that due to patient confidentiality, we are not allowed to write anything about patients that isn't on an official document (yes, yes I see the irony with this book here). All this means, is that we bring in a lot more John Does without any history.

another crew had brought him in earlier that day, but he sobered up and left while waiting for a bed. He went and got drunk again and we picked him up just in time for his first bed to be ready. It was as if we had made a reservation.

Steve likes to drink Listerine. If you've ever wondered why Listerine is kept behind the cash in downtown drugstores, it's because so many homeless people drink it to get drunk. By the way, it isn't behind the cash to stop homeless people from buying it; it is kept there to stop them from stealing it.

So we get a call to Dundas Square for an unconscious male. Very few people deserve to be called unconscious. Basically, unless he was shot, your typical 'unconcious' patient is drunk. Dundas Square is at the corner of Yonge and Dundas, across the street from the Eaton Centre. As it is right downtown and very public, it will often be full of tourists wondering how we treat our most vulnerable citizens.

As we approach, we see that it is Steve Pain-in-the-ass-ie. There is some kind of street fair going on and there is a crowd of people with camera phones exercising a form of public policing and street democracy. They are all prepared to capture some abuse of power and bring down the emergency services. They are focusing on the cops, but I get caught in the cross-fire. I'm sure I'm on Youtube somewhere. If you Googled "drunk, Dundas Square, paramedic-didn't-want-to-give-him-a-hug" and got a hit, it would be me or one of my colleagues.

As I said, there are concerned people all around him, but nobody is helping him to stand up. They are all concerned for his welfare and that his rights are not abused, but nobody actually wants to touch him. We pick up Mr. Pain-in-the-ass-ie and his Listerine bottle falls from his jacket. We leave it there. A concerned citizen tries to hand it to us.

"He dropped this. This is his."

My partner answers him, "That's what he got drunk on. He doesn't need any more of it." The person just stands there holding the Listerine as another person tries to get involved.

"That belongs to him. You should give it to him."

The person holding the Listerine bottle answers him, "The paramedics think he put alcohol into the bottle and that's what he's been drinking."

"It smells like Listerine."

Again my partner answers, "No, it *is* Listerine. He was drinking it and now he's drunk on Listerine."

The people only look at us blankly. Whether it is a look of surprise or disbelief, I'm not sure. Either way, I'm not particularly interested in what they think.

As we walk away we can hear the man announcing, "Does anyone want a bottle of Listerine?"

I could practically hear the doors swing open at Seaton House.

Response Priorities

We measure the severity of a call based on the information provided by the caller and interpreted by the call-taker at dispatch. This information is then sent to the paramedics and labeled Alpha, Bravo, Charlie, Delta, or Echo. If you were paying attention, you'd notice that it follows the alphabet. The lowest priority is Alpha and increases as you go on. Delta used to be our highest priority, but some medics weren't taking it seriously enough so they added Echo to make it sound scarier and motivate us to move faster.

Alpha - The lowest priority. This includes stubbed toes, minor cuts, cold and flu-like symptoms and people feeling lonely.

Bravo – This includes uncomplicated broken bones, a seizure that has stopped, psychiatric issues like depression where the patient has done nothing to harm him or herself, abdominal pain below the naval and minor bleeds.

Charlie - The same as the Bravos but worse and more serious in nature. It also includes abdominal pain above the naval and any Alpha if the patient has a history of heart problems.

Delta – This includes active seizures, chest pain, shortness of breath, uncontrolled bleeds, decreased level of awareness, and overdoses of any kind, including being drunk.

Echo – The highest priority. This includes choking, drowning, and cardiac arrests or any dead people (VSAs) who aren't Code-5.

Generally we only run lights and sirens to the patient if it is a Charlie, Delta or Echo. The reason we don't blaze everywhere is because it is a great risk to ourselves, the public, and the vehicle to go through red lights, even if you follow the Ambulance Act. Recently, we were running lights and sirens to a Delta cardiac arrest when we witnessed a car T-bone another one right in front of us. This is what happens when one car yields, as they should, and the other isn't paying attention. We had to stop and render first aid, which meant we had to call another ambulance to take care of Mr. Heartattack. This situation sucked for everyone involved.

We can run, or not run, any call we want. I've run Alphas because we were especially far away, it was a kid, the call information seemed to warrant it or because I felt like it. In the end it is always the paramedic's discretion, but you have to be prepared to justify it in coroner's court when you've run over a mother pushing a stroller while you were on your way to a patient with a blocked g-tube.

I'm Going to Retire Now

We got a call at 3:00 AM for a female unconscious in the hallway of a very nice apartment building in the Beaches. I would say 'The Beach', but then you might think that I'm from there. My partner, Candy·, and I have worked together fairly often and have a good rapport.

When we arrive, there are two cabs and a police car already parked outside. We walk in to find the cabbies with the police waiting in the front foyer for a superintendent to let them in. The super arrives and lets us all in to the building while the situation is explained to me.

The first cabbie brought home a young woman who was really drunk. Like, *really* drunk. Coyote-ugly-drunk. He helped her walk into the building and when she got to her door she realized that she didn't have her purse, so she had no money for the cab and no keys to get in to her apartment. While she is processing this information, she passes out on the floor in front of her door. The cabbie doesn't know what to do so he leaves her there on the floor and goes downstairs to call 911.

Meanwhile, her friends back at the bar have realized that she left her purse behind, so they take a second cab to join her at home. The second cabbie says he dropped them off outside the building. He was just leaving as the police arrived.

Because the girl was unconscious and 911 was called, we need to make sure that she is all right and hasn't

---

· Yes, yes a name that is commonly associated with strippers and prostitutes, but it's her real name, and she is neither. She's lovely and wholesome and... well, she's not a stripper or a prostitute anyway. Today we were joking about calling her Cinnamon (after her cinnamon addiction), but gave up when we realized it was actually *less* porno than her real name.

overdosed or anything. We go to the hallway, but she is gone. We don't know what happened to her. Her friends may have found her, let her in to her apartment and tucked her into bed or she may have been abducted by a man who lives across the hall (and would later be described as "quiet and kept to himself") while she was unconscious in the hallway. Currently she may be having ads posted on the internet which read, "Female 22 available, probably cute when vomit is brushed out of her hair."

The call turns into a 'check address' to confirm her wellbeing. We knock on the door, but there is no answer. The police bang on the door in the way that only cops can, but still no answer. We decide to go in with the help of the super, who is now the Key-Master·.

The super unlocks the door. We tell him to wait outside. It is dead quiet. The apartment is clean and well furnished. We call from the doorway, but there is no answer. We enter slowly, calling out and identifying ourselves continuously. No answer. We work our way to the bedroom. We knock on the door. We call out again. Nothing.

We open the bedroom door and from the doorway we can see a huddled mass under the sheet. We call out again, but this time the mass de-huddles itself and springs from the bed to standing. She is obviously and justifiably startled. She bounces quickly from foot-to-foot while nervously shaking her hands from side-to-side in front of her shoulders. I am attempting to reassure her as to who we are and why the four of us are standing in her bedroom, but she is barely listening. She is too surprised by our sudden presence to really process what I am saying. I look over at

---

· I love this term. Although it sounds very Lord of the Rings, it's actually from Ghostbusters.

the cops and they are also too surprised to hear anything I've been saying. I can't get her attention to help her focus. She, however, has our complete attention. I fall into silence as I appreciate what is before me.

She is in her early 20s, thin with black shoulder length hair and dark smooth flawless skin. She is only wearing a thong and a push up bra. Her breasts are full and round; such perfection could only have been airbrushed into my mind. If I could only use one word to describe her it would be: so, so, so, *so, sooooo* hot.

In my mind I'm saying, "Well, obviously you're okay. So we can leave you. Sorry to bother you," but I just can't quite get the words out. With a start she suddenly notices that she isn't wearing very much as she stands before us. In an effort to cover herself, she reaches down to grab the sheet from the bed. With a great flourish akin to a magician pulling a sheet to reveal a glorious surprise, she reveals two other nubile gorgeous young women equally dressed, or more accurately equally undressed, but certainly equally created by God. The last two are spooning in the bed. This is what you would call a triage situation. The two additions to my fantasy are not stirring in the slightest, despite the room full of people in uniform.

So here we are, two male cops, myself and my attractive female partner, in a room with three barely clad drunken women and all I can think is, "shouldn't someone be cuing the porno music?"

This is how we normally divide up the workload. There are two paramedics in a truck and each has a different role on a call. There is the attendant and there is the driver. The attendant is responsible for the call and will make all the decisions and does most of the talking to the patient.

The driver does all of the assessments – blood pressure, pulse, bandaging an injury, etc. The driver, as is implied by the name, will also drive the vehicle and communicate with dispatch as needed. We alternate these roles after every call to make it fair.

I drove the truck to this call, so it should be my partner's turn to attend and ask the patient all the questions. My partner turns to me, punches me in the arm and says, "Morgan, I'm going to let you attend *and* do all the assessments. Happy birthday." Normally, it is a punishment to make your partner do both, or it is a favour that you ask of them when you are too tired to do either. In this case, it is truly an act of selfless kindness for which I will be forever indebted.

"You're the best," I manage to stammer out.

Generally, my policy is that if they have been drinking, but can walk or if they are at home and someone can take care of them, they don't need a hospital. My real worry is them falling down or wandering into traffic. I've been drunker than most of my patients and never been to a hospital.

They are already safely in bed, so I decide that if I can wake them, it will be good enough. I climb into bed with them and try to wake them. *Sigh*. There are two good methods for causing someone pain in order to wake them up. One is the trap-squeeze, which is where you pinch the trapezoidal muscle, which runs over the shoulder; the other is called the sternal-rub. In a sternal-rub, one makes a fist and grinds your knuckles into the sternum of the patient. Both cause pain and will wake up a patient, whether they are legitimately sleeping or they are faking it. The sternum, as some of you may be aware, is located between the breasts. *Longer sigh.*

This isn't entirely the opportunity that some of you might be thinking. Using my role as a rescuer to touch the breast of a patient who is drunk-unconscious is an extremely high level of opportunistic rape. It is both immoral and criminal. Taking advantage of a person in this position never crosses my mind. If anything, it is the opposite. This kind of call is a career killer. A medic only needs one complaint from any of the people in the room that he or she is unprofessional and that medic is off the road pending a criminal investigation. The two cops present are actually a comfort to me as witnesses that I have remained professional and appropriate at all times. All this said, I wouldn't trade this call for any call in the world. I approach it with zeal and fearlessness.

So I give a little trap-squeeze here, a little sternal-rub there. One woman wakes pretty easily, but the other is really out. I can't get more than a moan from her, and believe me, I sternal-rubbed like there was no tomorrow.

"Did she take any drugs this evening?" I ask the woman who is still standing. "You can tell me the truth. The cops aren't here to arrest anyone. They just want to make sure everyone is safe. I promise you, the *last* thing they care about right now is arresting anyone." This is very true. We could have been standing in a meth-lab and the cops wouldn't have taken their eyes off the patient to arrest anybody.

"No, no drugs," she answers in a profoundly sexy Spanish accent. I mean *really* sexy. Bond-girl sexy. Centerfold sexy. Mmmmm[·]...

"Only drink," she continues. "She just break up with her boyfriend, so we get a little drunk." She says this as she slowly climbs back into bed and begins spooning the back of the currently spooning pair in bed. This makes her the new biggest spoon in this kitchen set of my dreams or the bread in a hot Latina sandwich. Once she is into full spooning position, she starts lightly stroking her friend, starting at her shoulder and gently running her fingers down her arm to her hips and continuing along down her thigh to the tips of her toes and then back up again. "She just break up with her boyfriend and she's so lonely. We just get a little drunk, because she's so... lo-o-o-nely."

I cannot put into words how much I love my job at this moment. I am thinking to myself that I have the greatest job in the world. There are a few more things running through my mind at this point, but this isn't the most appropriate place to share them. Many of them are already published in letters to Penthouse Forum. I'm already shaping my own letter in my mind, "Dear Xaviera Hollander, I've read these letters for a long time, but I never thought it would happen to me. I work in an unnamed urban city as a paramedic. One day we got a call..."

Perhaps it is just all the people in the room, but it starts to get really warm. Everyone is in stunned silence, except for my partner, she looks disappointed in the male species and says, "You *boys* finish this call and I'll be outside." She said 'boys' like it's a bad thing.

I was still pretty new at the time, and didn't appreciate that this was the call of a lifetime. I thought that

---

[·] I should really stop reminiscing and get back to the story.

this was going to be a regular perk to the job and that gorgeous, buxom Latinas would be naked before me on a regular basis. If I had known that nothing even close to this would ever happen to me again, I would have lingered a little longer. I would have put on the cardiac monitor and done a full secondary and complete neurological assessment, checking for equal chest rise and fall, limb drift (both arms and, oh yes, both legs), palpated the neck, spine, all four quadrants of the abdomen and every other thing I could think of. I might even have asked her if she had had a recent breast exam and did she want me to talk her through it. I certainly could have called for ALS back-up and had a crew indebted to me for life, but I chickened out.

Alas, I was new and (truth be told) shy, so I left after giving advice about sleeping in the recovery position and calling back if we are needed. I was tempted to tell them that I got off at 7:00 AM, if she was still feeling lonely, but I had a feeling that they wouldn't be up for breakfast.

The two cops and I float out of the room in a dream-state with soft smiles etched onto our faces. My partner was still waiting in the hallway, looking bored, but we are oblivious. We are silently sharing the moment, like hikers awestruck by a gorgeous sunset at the end of a long and tiring journey. Only this sunset has legs that would put wood on a statue.

Of the two policemen·, one was much older than the other. "I'm going to retire now," he announces as much to himself as to the rest of us. "That's it. I'm done tonight. I'm putting in my papers. I am supposed to retire next

---

· Yes, yes the proper term is Police *Officer*, but I really want to impress the maleness of the scenario. Besides, I am so digging the footnotes. I'm going to go back to the beginning of the book and add footnotes, all willy-nilly-like, everywhere I can.

month, but fuck it, I'll take the penalty. I want this to be the last call I do. I want this to be the last memory I have of this job. I'm leaving with this image in my mind. I don't care. This is my gift to myself. I retire as soon as I walk out this door."

The best part of this story is that he really did retire that day.

Elderly, HTN and on Blood thinners

We got an Alpha for an elderly woman with a nose bleed. This may not sound serious to you, but some of the worst bleeds I've ever seen were elderly people with high blood pressure taking blood thinners. Taking blood thinners means that their blood won't clot and the high blood pressure means that it flows just a little stronger. This makes for a messy combination and can be hard to stop. A nose bleed can be pretty serious because it is usually impossible to apply direct pressure. Yes, yes you can pinch the nose like your Mother said you should, but the blood will sometimes run down your throat and cause you to vomit. Vomiting blood really raises some eyebrows, not to mention blood pressure.

We arrived on scene and saw that a response-car was parked outside. A response car, or zoom car, is a single medic in a Jeep Tahoe. He or she can't transport a patient, but the idea is that they can get there first and stabilize the patient or cancel the transport crew if an ambulance is unnecessary. They are never caught up in offload delay because they never transport so they are always available. They are also handy as an extra pair of hands for lift assists or cardiac arrests.

Hopefully the response medic has done all the assessments (read as: work) and we can just act as a transport unit and drive away. We climb the stairs and see the patient sitting on the toilet. There is blood all over her shirt and all over the bathroom. We breathe a sigh of relief as we see that she is fully clothed and is only using the toilet as a bench. It is the same situation described above: elderly, blood thinners and hypertension. The only thing that is a little different is that on her nose, the response guy has MacGyvered up a little gadget.

He has taken two tongue depressors and wrapped tape around the ends to make them into a clip like a clothes peg. He has then fitted the clip over her the bridge of her nose. It looks ridiculous, but seems to work. Things look pretty under control, so we simply carry the woman down the stairs and head off to the hospital. I'm thinking that I'm a little wiser for having seen such a clever little trick.

At Mt. Sinai we are being triaged when I notice my partner do a fast double take at the patient. I look up to see what he was looking at and I also do the same double take. As I slowly approach the patient, I can see blood trickling from her eyes. Thin bright red liquid is gently rolling down her cheeks. The blood has filled her sinus cavities and found its escape through her eye sockets. It looks biblical. I am witnessing Stigmata. She doesn't appear to be in any distress as she softly dabs at her cheeks.

"Are you okay?" I ask.

"Yes, I'm fine," she replies. "It's just that my eyes won't stop tearing."

I gesture for the triage nurse's attention. She gives the patient a similarly startled look and then gets us a bed.

Endings

When I talk to non-medics about a call I did for a sick person, they always have the same hopeful look in their eyes when they ask, "So what happened to the patient?" I don't want to answer, because I know the reaction I'll get when I say, "He died" or "She'll never wake up again" or "He'll probably be paralyzed" or "That was the last time she'll ever be in her own home" or "So they never got to say goodbye". No one likes a sad ending and I think we get so used to American movies that it gets really hard to handle one in real life. There was a good line in a film[1] where someone European says something to the effect of, "The problem with you Americans is that you always expect things to work out well, while most of the world knows that it usually won't."[2] Anyone who deals in emergency or medical services knows this first hand.

People in the health care field think differently about death and illness than others. We treat emergencies like a job and keep our emotions to ourselves. It isn't that we don't care about the patients, we do, but I will say that your self-esteem can't be based on the outcome of your patients. It's just a survival technique for us. It doesn't mean I don't want to tell you how the patient fared, feel free to ask – just be prepared for the answer to not be a Hollywood Christmas-Special-Miracle ending. Remember the rules at the beginning of the book?

---

[1] I've forgotten the name of the film and I wouldn't mind an email if you happen to know.

[2] Turns out it wasn't a film, it was an episode of The Sopranos. Season 4, episode 10. The one-legged Russian woman says to Tony, "That's the trouble with you Americans. You expect nothing bad ever to happen, when the rest of the world expect only bad to happen and they are not disappointed."

Rule #1: People die.
Rule #2: You can't always change Rule #1.

One Friday night I was working in the core. A friend was having a party downtown so we basically made it our standby location for the night. After every call we'd go back to the party instead of going to our station. Before we left we would tell people what the call was for and then we'd come back afterwards and people would ask how it went. Almost every call so far that night was for a drunk person (it was warm Friday night after all), and almost every patient refused to go to the hospital; the calls were all benign and nobody was really hurt.

At 2:45 am we get a call for a man who fainted in his home. It comes in as a Charlie. We tell a few people at the party that we are off to a 'fainting' and we drive away.

The story is that the patient woke up at 2:30 in the morning to go to the bathroom. His wife heard a thud, found him unconscious on the floor and called 911. We walk into the bedroom and he's blue in the face. We check a pulse and he's dead. We try to shock him but it's too late. When we returned to the party, people lightly asked us how he was. When we bluntly replied that he died, people became visibly upset. They didn't know him, they weren't the ones doing CPR and they didn't have to face his wife, but it still affected them. It was a real party killer.

Closer from SummerWorks 2008

When Paramedics tell each other stories, we almost always leave out the ending. Whether the patient lives or dies can't be what it is all about. The biggest reason that we don't talk about patient outcome is because most often, we don't know. We wheel them into the hospital and give our report to Triage. They had a pulse when we left. End of story.

Another major reason is that you can't start keeping score of your wins and losses; if you take credit for the lives saved, you have to take responsibility for the lives lost and nobody wants to do that.

For me, thinking whether the patient lives or dies can't be the focus during treatment. People die. That is just a fact. I know that my skills, my training and my treatment are only three factors in a big picture of what it will take to save this person's life. One of the biggest factors is time, including how long it takes to get to the patient. The public would be outraged to know how often I've been the only available ambulance left in the south-east quadrant. That means that every other ambulance was already with a patient: either on scene, in transport or, most likely, in offload delay in a hospital.

Recently, my partner and I were at Bloor and Sherbourne when we got a Delta to Bathurst and Finch for a child with difficulty breathing. From Bloor and Sherbourne, we were the closest available ambulance in the entire city. It took us 17 minutes of driving lights and sirens to get to a child who couldn't breathe. That is shameful.

We need more ambulances to keep the city safe. Twice a week for six weeks in the summer of 2008, paramedics wore yellow shirts that said, "More Ambulances. More Paramedics. More Lives Saved." We wore these to create dialogue with the public and to raise awareness of the lack of paramedic resources in the city. You won't see those shirts anymore. Management told us to stop wearing them, subject to a disciplinary offence if we didn't comply. You can make your own conclusions about what that says about communication in our organization.

This ends my public service announcement. Just when you thought you had a book that wasn't political.

Closer at The Fringe 2009

You may have noticed that there is a strike going on with the City of Toronto. EMS is not an essential service (Fire and Police are both essential, but, contrary to public belief and common sense, ambulance isn't.) so it means that we are caught up in this strike. The biggest issue for paramedics is sick-time. I want to be clear that we aren't asking for anything new in this contract; we just don't want to lose what we already have.

We have a good sick plan.

We get one paid sick day per month and, if we don't use it, have the ability to accumulate them over our career. The City wants to take these single paid sick days away from us, as well as not paying out a portion of unpaid sick days at the end of our career.

I just want to throw a few things out for you to think about. We get exposed to a lot on our job. The most obvious thing is germs. When someone calls 911 because they aren't feeling well (which is a call we get every day), we go into their home where they have been coughing, sneezing, vomiting, bleeding and had diarrhea. We don't know if they are not feeling well from: common flu, swine flu, Norwalk, SARS, Ebola or whatever the next killer virus will be.

In the winter, I got a call for a young healthy guy who suddenly dropped dead. As I'm doing CPR, he starts pouring blood from his mouth. Every time I do a chest compression he sprays blood at me. I'm getting it on my arms, my face and it is soaking my shirt. We bring him to the hospital where he gets pronounced DOA. I wash my face and arms. I go back to the station where I change out of my bloody uniform and put on a fresh one. I finish the rest of my shift and do more calls. At the end of my shift, I go home, hug my kids and put them to bed.

Three days later, I get a call from Public Health to say that the patient had died from flesh eating disease of the lungs. The reason that there was so much blood was that that the disease had devoured into his pulmonary arteries. They tell me that I had had an extreme exposure to necrotizing fasciitis and that I needed to start anti-biotics immediately before I became symptomatic within 5 days of exposure. This was the evening of day three.

A medic friend of mine is off the road for a month because of the severe side effects from taking the antiretroviral cocktail after a patient with HIV and HEP-C threw up in his eyes and mouth. Yes, the chances of contracting HIV are small, but that is cold comfort when it is your own health; also, if he didn't take the cocktail, he would be denied health benefits if he developed either disease anytime for the rest of his life.

The disconcerting part for me was that that was supposed to be my call. He was on nights and I was on days; the call came in at 6:30 am and I offered to do it for him. He declined because it was just 'waking up a drunk' and it should have been a simple, straight-forward call. Now he's off the road for a month while he's sick from the medication.

Yes, we have a good sick plan. We need a good sick plan*.

This job gets harder and harder the longer you do it. I'm expected to do this job until I'm 63 years old to get a pension; something tells me I'll need more sick days at the end of my career than I need now.

The longer you work, the more emotional calls that you experience will create triggers off the job; and the longer you live, the more experiences from life will create emotional triggers on the job.

I probably do a stroke every few weeks. I don't find them scary or stressful calls, but a while ago I did a call for an elderly Ukrainian man who was having an obvious and severe stroke. I was speaking broken Ukrainian to the patient and to his family and I realized that I was getting way too emotionally involved.

---

* In January of 2010, I was stuck with the needle of a junkie, just after he had used it to shoot up and OD. This is much, much higher risk. I'm having a crap month. Shitty, shitty doughnuts. FML.

The call should have been the same as any other stroke, however my Ukrainian father-in-law had died suddenly in an accident a few weeks before. During the call, I realized that I really needed this patient to live –for me. I felt like if he lived, it would give me some kind of redemption with my father-in-law, however, if he died it would be like losing my father-in-law all over.

I was shaking and close to tears as I desperately asked him to squeeze my hands. I finished the call, but just barely and it drained me. For anyone else, or for me at any other time, this wouldn't have been an emotional call, but for me, at that moment, it was almost too much to handle.

My own father was recently diagnosed with cancer and given a couple years to live·. Now, every time I have a patient with end-stage cancer, I picture my dad. And when I'm with my dad, I can picture my patients who were at the ends of their lives.

Every paramedic will go on stress leave. It's a given. We prepare for it in school and go into the job knowing it. Whether we need 2 hours, a day, a week, a year or it ends our career –every paramedic will get that call which is just too much and we need a break.

We aren't asking for anything new in this contract. We just don't want to lose what we have. Believe me, you don't want a paramedic coming for you or a family member who is unfit to work physically, mentally or emotionally but still comes to work anyway because he or she can't afford an unpaid sick day.

· He actually passed away within 6 months.
John F. Phillips October 17, 1945 – January 2, 2010.
RIP, I miss you Dad.

Yes, we have a good sick plan. We need a good sick plan. We deserve a good sick plan·.

· So after 6 weeks, the strike ended in August of 2009. We lost our existing sick plan, but in my opinion, we got a better one. The big loss is not being able to cash out unused sick days at the end of our career, but in the new plan we are given enough sick days to reach Long Term Disability (which we didn't have before). Certainly, in the event of a major injury (ask Kevin Mills) it is a better plan.

Glossary

10-4 – Yeah, ok.
10-6 – "Standby, I'm busy." This is something a dispatcher would say to you on the radio while they are on a landline.
10-7 – Not available by trunk radio. Or, we have arrived wherever we were going.
10-8 – Available by trunk radio. Or, we're on our way to wherever we are going.
10-9 – Patient on board.
10-13 –"I can't tell you that right now." You would say that when you are asked a question on the air that you don't want to answer in front of someone like a family member because the answer would upset them.
10-19 – Go back to your station.
10-20 – Your location.
10-23 – We are at our standby location. Most medics don't know this one and dispatchers will be impressed if you can use it in a sentence.
10-26 – Being cancelled from whatever assignment you were about to do.
10-32 – Medic down or severely injured.
10-33 – Big emergency worth interrupting other people's transmissions on the radio.
10-90 – Ten-ninety or Ninety. Meal break. Lunch is a 30 minute break between hour 4 and hour 7.5 of a 12-hour shift. Given shift work, this break happens at all hours, but is always called lunch. This is our only scheduled break and can still be interrupted to service a call.
10-200 – The police. AKA the two hundreds or the twos.
10-2000 – A paramedic's life is in danger and police are needed in a major rush.
211 – Two-eleven. A person having a psychiatric emergency. Also known as EDP.

40 Station – The ambulance station downtown at Church and Richmond.
45 Station – The ALS/CBRN station at Bay and Davenport. AKA The Kennel because of their proficiency at fucking the dog. Members of this station created and live by such slogans as "embrace the decay" and "apathy will set you free." They manage to avoid doing calls as they prepare for "the big one". If things go bad, I wouldn't want to be one of them. Until then, it's a pretty sweet gig.
799 – Seven-nine-nine. The helicopter. Working down town makes it hard to justify ever calling for it, but I've heard of it done for calls on the 401 with multiple patients and traffic gridlock.
911 – The phone number one dials in North America☎ to reach the big 3 emergency services. In Australia it is 000. New Zealand is 111. Most of Europe is 112 (Norway is 113, Belarus is 103, etc,). China is 120. Japan is 119. India is 108. You should really ask locally and not trust me with this kind of thing.·
ACP – See ALS
ACR – Ambulance Call Report. This was/is the paperwork that we fill out after every patient contact. It details everything that happened during the call and all of the patient's medical history. It takes about twenty minutes. It has been replaced with the E-PCR.
AKA – Also Known As.

☎ Interesting fact: In 1959, Winnipeg, Manitoba became the first city in North America to get 911. It was 9 more years before the first American city began using it.

· This is me anticipating an international market. I firmly believe that if it is more accessible, it will be enjoyed by more people and that can only mean more… money.

ALS or ACP – Advanced Life Support or Advanced Care Paramedic. These are the paramedics with advanced training who are able to give many more life saving drugs than the lowly BLS medics.

BLS or PCP – Basic Life Support or Primary Care Paramedic. This is the starting level paramedic. We can give 6 life saving drugs and are valued for our use of Accelerator Therapy. This type of care was previously known as Diesel Therapy until the trucks all went to gasoline. Gas therapy gives another connotation that we avoid, so we focus on our masterful use of the pedal.

BOB – Bed, Oxygen, Blanket. The cornerstone treatment of EMS.

BVM – Bag Valve Mask. The apparatus we use to breathe for a patient who either isn't breathing on their own or is breathing ineffectively.

CBRNE – AKA Glow Worm Medics. I believe this stands for Chemical, Biological, Radioactive, Nuclear, Explosive. Four things I prefer to avoid on the job.

D-tank – Oxygen tank, or O2 for giving oxygen to the patients. Same idea as a SCUBA tank. Makes an excellent bludgeoning tool.

E-PCR – Electronic Patient Care Report or as we call it, "E-Pecker". This replaced the ACR for documenting patient care. It is a very expensive piece of electronics that is the size of a very thick laptop. It is more widely used now, but for the longest time was only used as a hard writing surface to fill out paper ACRs.

EDP – Emotionally Disturbed Person. This is more of a Police term for 211.

FML – Fuck My Life. A line coined from Super Bad. Later turned into a terrific website and book.

FNG – Fucking New Guy. See Newbie. This sounds harsh, but is not necessarily a pejorative term.

FOOSH – Fall On Out-Stretched Hand. AKA a Colles' fracture or a 'parking lot fracture' because it happens while walking to your car and slipping on ice. My Californian cousin sustained one of these while visiting me in the winter of 2010. I had warned him that a certain path near my house was called "Colles' Fracture Alley". As we entered the path, I was explaining the concept of walking on ice when he slipped, fell and broke his wrist thus sustaining a colles' fracture. The worst part is that I had never called it "Colles' Fracture Alley" before; I was only kidding.

FTO – Field Training Officer. AKA preceptor. An FTO is a medic who has a student assigned to him or her for on-the-road training. After seven years, I had the seniority to become an FTO, but by then I was unable to pass the written test because I had forgotten everything from school. Cursed irony.

GAS – Gravity, Alcohol, Stupidity. This is the source of ninety-nine percent of all calls. If your call doesn't fit into one of these categories, you aren't looking hard enough.

GCS – Glasgow Coma Scale. The scale to determine or explain the degree of LOA. GCS increases from 3 (dead) to 15 (perky and fully alert).

GP – General Public. People without medical backgrounds who, through years of watching medical TV shows, have strong opinions about patient care. The number one source of complaints.

HBD – Has Been Drinking. A drunk person. Boozer. I would say a lush, but that has another connotation.

HTN – Hypertension. High blood pressure. Often when you ask a patient if they have high blood pressure, they say "no" but when you go through their medication you find four different blood pressure meds. You bring this to their attention and they say, "Oh, well I used to have high blood pressure, but now I take medication, so not anymore."

LOA – Level Of Awareness. How conscious the person is.
LOC – Loss Of consciousness. Getting knocked out.
MID – Muffin In Distress. Someone who clearly does not need an ambulance and is making a much bigger deal of the situation than is warranted.
NEA – Non-Emergency Ambulance. See PCTU for full definition. NEA could also stand for Not Even an Ambulance or No Emergencies Allowed, No Electrical Activity, Nice Elderly Ambulance driver or Never Ever Available.
OD – Over dose. Taking a dangerous amount of any drug or medication.
OLD – Offload Delay. See below for full definition.
PC Number – Police Constable Number. Badge number.
PCP – See BLS
PI – Car accident. I'm not sure what PI actually stands for. Personal Injury? Property Involved? Premium Increase? Problematic Insurance? Particularly Irritating? Pretty Impaired? Potentially Insane? People Incompetent? Part-time Ignoramus? Petty Issue? Partly Imbecilic? Persistently Inconsiderate? Passably Intelligent? Panicking Individual? Probably Irrelevant? Pretty Insignificant? Peace Interrupted? Pain In the…?
PCTU – Patient Care Transfer Unit. AKA NEA. Non-emergency transfer crews. These crews would bring people from the hospital back home once they are less ill or they could bring people from home to hospital for diagnostic tests or treatments. They also transfer people from one hospital to another. This is a gig generally occupied by people with the highest seniority because there are no nights or weekends and the environment is always safe and stable. When the car count gets too low, they will be asked to do emergency calls. This never goes over well.
SOB – Short Of Breath.

VSA – Vital Signs Absent. A dead person.
Apical pulse – Measuring the pulse rate by listening directly to the heart for sound with a stethescope.
Backstage Pass – TEMS uniform in a certain context, perhaps at a certain Broken Social Scene concert...
Bag a patient – The act of squeezing the BVM and breathing for them. This is so named because a BVM has a big plastic bag full of oxygen on the end of it. I clarify this because someone once pointed out to me that 'bagging a patient' sounds very Sopranos; like I've put a plastic bag over someone's head and am suffocating them. This is a practice we are forbidden from doing. When a patient is especially stinky/pooey, we will essentially "bag" them by cutting arm and leg holes and arranging plastic bags to seal them up.
Booze Formula – However many drinks the person said they had, double it and add 6 to find the actual consumption.
Or if x = stated beers, and y = actual beers then $2x + 6 = y$.
C-Spine – The part of your spine from the base of your skull to your shoulders. AKA your neck. The C stands for cervical which, to this day, I can't say without blushing.
Circle of Healing – When the firefighters stand around the patient while waiting for the ambulance to arrive and actually do something useful. AKA the Stare of Life.
Code 5 – Very, very dead. Obviously dead. Not worth trying to attempt to save.
Code Brown – Pt is at severe risk of imminent bowel movement on the stretcher.
Code Yellow – Same as above with urine.
The Core – Downtown, Yonge St. around The Eaton Centre. Generally, Sherbourne to University and Bloor to King. Most non-core medics avoid it like the plague. If you are from any other part of the city and bring a patient into a core hospital, it's virtually impossible to get out

again. The downtown call volume is so high that you just keep getting calls as you clear the hospital on your way back to your station. Because you are in the core, you keep bringing them back to downtown hospitals. It is a never-ending cycle that is called 'getting sucked into the core.' The funny thing is that, we in the core, get inescapably sucked into the North West and we hate it just as much. There should be some kind of exchange program like they have for prisoners or hostages so we could both get back to our own quadrant.

Courtesy Call – These are calls where some kind of assistance is required, but the caller knows full well that it isn't an emergency and that they won't be going to the hospital. Most often this comes in the form of a lift assist. Generally, we don't mind these.

Darwin Award – This is the award given to someone that does something so stupid that they lose their ability to reproduce (usually by death) and thus make for a healthier gene pool.

Dr. Summersoff – Any MD who will provide you with a note that explains an illness and allows you to miss work so that you can 'rest' in the summer.

Dr. Wintersoff – Same as previous, except for people who like to ski.

Dyspnea – Difficulty breathing. We measure the degree of difficulty breathing by how many words the patient can say between breaths. So, if after every three words they need to take a breath, we'd call it three-word dyspnea.

Emerge – The Canadian term for The Emergency Room. Many people call it the ER, which is the American term made famous by some TV show that I forget the name of.

EMS – Emergency Medical Services. Once upon a time, it was Earn Money Sleeping, but those days are long gone.

When I'm grumpy, it's Earn My Stretcher. Could also be Eat My Shorts.

Exsanguination – Losing all your blood. This is bad and generally leads to death.

Fire – Firefighters, Smoke Jockeys. You would never hear me saying Hose Monkeys; that would be rude.

Forty-Word-Dyspnea – This is a condition where the patient claims to be short of breath, but won't shut up long enough for you to be able to assess them.

Flight 7:01 – Flight Seven-O-One or The Miracle of 19:01. At 7:01 am and 7:01 pm (19:01 on the 24 hr clock) crews across the city that are still in a hospital will simultaneously finish cleaning their stretchers and completing their paperwork so that they can clear from the hospital. Coincidentally, these times occur at the end of our shift and we can no longer be given a call while driving back to our station thus securing that we go home on time.

Gorked out – Permanently vegetative state. Either by over- medication, old age or brain injury.

Hini – *Rhymes with "whiney"*, AKA H1N1. Formerly called Swine Flu until the Pork Industry got mad. This is either the most over-hyped profit driven illness in history or an underestimated pandemic that will cause phenomenal heartbreak and devastation. The jury is still out, as am I. I go back and forth between saying, "It's a flu, get over it." And "Holy shit, that guy died?!"

Incarceritis – When someone faces incarceration for a crime and develops chest pain or SOB to delay going to jail. This medical emergency can happen at any stage along the road to imprisonment, but often occurs at the time of arrest. Common in shoplifters. Perhaps caused by an allergy to handcuffs.

Lift Assist – Quite literally lifting someone (with no injuries) from the ground and putting him or her in a chair, in a bed or just back on their feet. This is your classic, "I've fallen and I can't get up." They aren't hurt; they just tripped and can't get up on their own. The patient is either alone or with a life partner who is too old to pick the patient up on their own*.

Listerine – Any brand of mouthwash when consumed to get drunk. I wanted to organize a Stumblefest with a 5-drink minimum where everyone *had* to leave falling down. People were into the idea until I mentioned that we could all do a round of Listerine shooters. At this point the evening was cancelled and I was deemed too dangerous to invite out to parties anymore.

Major – The area of the Emerge that deals with Major medical problems. This is where very sick people go.

Medic – Paramedic.

Methadone – An extremely addictive drug given by rehab programs to treat heroin and opiate addiction. Methadone is a really hard drug to kick. I have heard of many people who go back on heroin to try and get off methadone. Ironically, heroin was invented by the Bayer Company to treat morphine addiction. Morphine was created by Serturner and Company to treat opium addiction and alcoholism. Amazingly, pharmaceutical companies get away with having the government pay for a drug which treats the last drug they invented to treat another drug they created to treat the abuse of a socially acceptable beverage that the government collects tax on. Does no one else see

---

* Cate Friesen has a wonderful song called *Passionately Fond of You,* about a very elderly couple. The line "I will be your eyes and you can steady me" has always been a favorite of mine. We see this all the time in elderly couples; it's generally pretty adorable.

the pattern and lack of incentive on the part of pharmaceutical companies and government to actually solve this problem?

Monday Call – This call can happen on any day of the week. It is any "emergency" where the patient delayed calling 911 so as not to interfere with something going on in their personal life.

Newbie – Newly hired person in their first year.

Offload Delay – AKA Offload Decay. When paramedics sit with a patient on their stretcher in the hallway of Emergency before the hospital takes responsibility for them. Offload delay can take hours. My personal record is eleven hours of offload delay in one shift. This was divided between two patients. Six and a half hours at Toronto Western and four and a half at East General. As a further insult to the soul crushing experience of sitting in a hallway and staring at a patient, we get a page from dispatch every 20 minutes that states our status as, "still OLD".

Paramedic – The people who respond to medical 911 calls and take people to the hospital via ambulance. At this point in reading this book, you should be painfully familiar with this term.

The Portable – The walkie-talkie-like radio that we carry around outside of the truck.

Privates – The for-profit non-emergency businesses that do first-aid at special events or non-emergency transfers of patients. The vehicles have lights and sirens, but they aren't allowed to use them. They're just for show. There is also a genital joke here that I will refrain from making.

Response Car – Zoom Car. Or simply, Response. A single medic in a Chevy Tahoe who gets to the scene first and begins patient care while waiting for a transporting ambulance.

Resusc – Resuscitation Room in the Emerge. This is where the sickest people go. This should not be confused with "recess", although I have seen medics write that on ACRs.
Rubby – Homeless person. Generally with psychiatric or substance abuse issues. You wouldn't know it to read this, but I'm actually very respectful and understanding around issues of homelessness.
Rubby Down – A typical rubby-down call is phoned in by cell phone for a homeless person who is HBD. The caller is usually afraid to approach the patient, but is concerned for their well-being. They are usually cured with the "clap of life." They may or may not want to go to the hospital, but will always be urged to go by well-intentioned bystanders.
Rubsicle Season – Winter.
Running a call – Driving with lights and sirens. AKA sparking it up, flipping on the cherries, or getting there fast.
SARS – Sudden Acute Respiratory Syndrome. A very serious breathing disease that ravaged Toronto in March 2003. Twenty three thousand people were quarantined, 358 cases were confirmed and of those 38 died. The real concern from City Officials came as the tourist industry became threatened. For paramedics, many new precautions were introduced regarding wearing: masks, gowns, face shields, and double gloves. Medics in the South West said, "What is this bullshit?" Medics in the North East, where SARS originated, said, "Can we get those space suits that astronauts wear? Or at least those deep sea diving suits with the big helmets?"
Scrote – See Skid.
Shamewich – A sandwich that you get from the emerge department which is meant for the homeless.
Shit Magnet – Someone who, through no fault of their own, does an above average number of hot calls.

Skid –Someone who is obnoxious *and* currently has greater than three of the following: missing teeth, a mullet, multiple tattoos (homemade or prison tattoos count as double), a pitbull, deriving income by some illegal means *while* collecting social assistance, poor bathing habits, drug and alcohol addictions, acid wash jeans, lives in a shelter, their friends and family are mostly scrotes.
South East – The city is divided into 4 quadrants. The dividers being Yonge St. and Eglinton Ave. I work in the South East quadrant. This includes the Core.
Staging – To stage means to wait for the police before going into the call and making patient contact. The decision to stage is based on call information or patient history that indicates a possible danger to paramedics. We'll park the ambulance in a location where we can see the address, but (hopefully) the patient can't see us. If they see us first, it gets awkward. Staging is done for our safety.
Status Dramaticus – A chronic state of overdramatization. Often, but not necessarily, associated with patients who have a history of anxiety. This condition often increases in severity with the arrival of the ambulance in order to provoke guilt in witnesses and prove that the patient's suffering is justified. Often the chief complaint of an MID.
Sternal Rub – Rubbing your knuckles on the sternum (breast plate) of a patient to cause them pain and wake them when they are sleeping or "unconscious".
Tib-fib – Tibula/fibula. The bones connecting your knee to your foot.
Trap Squeeze – The pinching of the trapezius muscle (muscle between the shoulder and neck) to cause pain to a patient and wake them from "unconsciousness".
Traum-edy – When the call information states a major trauma, but when you arrive the actual injury is so minor that it makes you laugh.

Trigger – A call which touches you emotionally in a way that is stronger than you'd like it to be. These include: kids and calls that are too familiar to your own personal life.
Trunk Radio – The communication radio in the truck.
Unconscious – An overused term that usually means sleeping.
White Cloud – Someone who is lucky and doesn't tend to do hot calls. The opposite of a Shit Magnet.
Zebra Hunters – This is a term coined from this simple story: A bunch of student doctors are in a field on a ranch in Alberta when they hear galloping hooves, whinnying and neighing. The teacher asks, "What animal do you think is coming?" Most reply that it sounds like a horse, but one stands up and says, "Ah, but it could be a zebra." The Zebra Hunter is the one who chooses the least likely possible diagnosis, even when a very obvious and more likely one is before him. This is only really useful if you are a character on House.

Acknowledgements

I've always marveled at authors who dedicate their book to one person. How can they decide who that lucky person is? Aren't they worried about offending someone else? Sure, picking one person works great if you know that there will be another book later, but this might be my only shot at having a book printed. It was harder than I had planned. I'm not sure I've got another one in me.

In the beginning, I agonized for longer than I should have over deciding whether to dedicate it to my parents or my wife and children. Sophie's Choice all over again. Then I started thinking of all the other people I should thank. Of course, there were the people who helped me to edit the book and my partners. Then I started thinking of all my other friends, coworkers and people who were influential to my life in general. Then there were all the other role-model-types who I appreciated for making me the person who I am: my family, teachers, bosses, and other special friends. The list started growing. Anyone who bought earlier editions will have watched the evolution grow.

I had been trying desperately to keep the "Thank-Yous" to a minimum, when I suddenly realized that it's *my* book and I can do whatever I want with it. I have no one to answer to. Currently, no publisher, agent or editor to curb my enthusiasm. I had been making the font smaller and smaller, but now I'm just going to add pages. I don't care. So here, without explanation, is the beginning of a list of people who have meant something to me over the years. This is by no means a complete list and, like the book, will probably grow with each publication, but these are some of the people who, without thinking too hard, have gotten me to where I am today. When else am I going to get a chance to do something like this?

Additional Thanks,
Dr McCullough, Bennett, Jules, Nick, David P, Linda, Glen, Laurel, Sophia, Zola, Freya, Dan, Jean, Phil, Dave J, Kay, Tee, Lizzie, Mike, Frosty, Jessica, Allison, Baba, Dido, Kether B, Jonathan L, Seth, Ms Ots, George F, Margaret F, William P, Elizabeth F, Leigh T, Dan C, Dorothy J, LeRoy J, Pearl J, Talitha C-J, Adam C, Simon C, Brandy, Farley, Sweet-Pea, Sam, Puffy, Ginger, Mark G, Caleb R, Mila L, Brendhan D, Josh M, Don M, John , Marta LeG, Jos H, Jacob P, Haji N, David E, David U, (so many Davids), Adam S, Marni N, Allison S, Charles S, Ohad B, Mike K, Nick G, Dave M, Declan H, Doug M, Evalyn P, Norah L, Erik P, Colin M, Jason C, Matt B, Tom T, Brian S, Debbie B-M, Mr. Brindley, Mr. McLean, Dan A, John B, Jane C, Chevy C, Garrett M, Bill M, Gilda R, Lorraine N, Luc I, Julie S, Patty J, Rick, Deb, Zoe H, David F, Fiona H, Wolfgang V, Matt M, Keith, Patricia, Ilene and all at Peace Child, Martin A, Prabhat J, Michael L, Melanie B, Shatrupa D, Stefane C, Shailender, Jeremy M, Viji J, Marie-Eve P, Hetal, Tasleem H, Yashika, Jessica D, Devaki, David M, Diane M, Jim M, Ian M, all at CWY, Jay LeB, Richard Y, Julie, Peter G, Sting, Andy S, Stewart C, Mark C, Leesa H, Mary B, Sarah, Cherie M, Loree L, youth of KYTES, David B, Tina W, Chris F, Jerry H, Ed G, Duncan MacC, Lindsay M, Sarah Z, Mike A, Chuck S, Don H, Wendy, Jim M, John D, Ray M, Robbie K, Angela, Keith J, Billy Y, Sarah K, Sean M, Oscar P, Ed T, Ray B, Jaco P, Stanley C, Flea, Ron, Brian K, Dick F, Phil S, Dave H, Alayne M, Kim B, Mike M, Rob K, Mike H, Danny A, Toni A, Mike D, Allison R, Ornella G, Angelo de L, Johnny, Roy, Dr. Herer, W.P. K, Stuart McL, David M, William G, Farley M, Steve M, George C, Lenny B, Bill C, Woody A, Robin W, Bob N, Eddie M, Jim C, Corin R, Vince C.

Catherine "Kitty" Phillips, nee Turner
Aug 12, 1908 – Aug 17, 2011

Someone once said that everyone has a chance to be a hero. Not everyone will jump in front of a bullet or push someone out of the way of a speeding car, but we all have a chance to be helpful every day. Every one of us has an opportunity to make someone else's day better by being polite, respectful and thoughtful. By doing this, you make their life better and if everyone did this every day, the world would be a better place. What is a more appropriate definition of a hero than someone who makes the world a better place to live in?

My Grandma Kitty lived this philosophy. You couldn't identify a specific accomplishment that she achieved or brag about any event that she participated in, but she lived every day of her life being kind and thoughtful of others. She was an amazing person who outlived all of her friends and immediate family. Despite her being ready to go several years ago, I'm thankful that she hung around so that my kids were able to know her. Two of my kids have variations of her name as middle names (Catherine for Zoriana and Kit for Lukie)

I'll miss her quiet wisdom, tremendous patience, help with crosswords and her knitting. I liked something my cousin said in her obituary: "With all the changes and inventions over the last 103 years, her favorite was being able to buy pre-plucked chickens. Because, really what's a more useful innovation than that?" She lived to be 103 and was lucid for every one of them. She died peacefully in her sleep surrounded by family. After a lifetime of giving, she was certainly owed that.

Morgan Jones Phillips was born in The Baldwin St. Gallery of Photography in Toronto in 1971. He worked in collectively created theatre and many odd jobs for most of his life. For a few special years he was the Artistic Director of KYTES (Kensington Youth Theatre and Employment Skills). His first solo play, *The Emergency Monologues,* won the NOW Audience Choice Award at the SummerWorks Theatre Festival in 2008. He loves cycling, canoeing and is proud to be a humble Quaker. He lives in Riverdale with his wife and three children and has been a paramedic since 2003.

To book a show or for more information about The Emergency Monologues or just to chat, contact me at
morganjonesphillips@gmail.com
Or check out www.emergencymonologues.com
Or find Emergency Monologues on Facebook
Twitter @emergemonos

Originally from London, Ontario, **Vince Cheng** got into the medical field because he didn't get into art school. He has still kept up with his passion for illustration by drawing cartoons and designing medical themed shirts for charity. He also enjoys cooking, martial arts, teaching, travel and medical volunteerism. Vince has been an Emergency Nurse since 1999.

...and sometimes Vince will partake in pachinko while wearing his medical themed shirts.